the Ancient Power of Crystals

the ANCIENT POWER of CRYSTALS

HISTORY, LEGENDS, AND HEALING PRACTICES FROM AROUND THE WORLD

Philip Permutt

CICO BOOKS

Published in 2025 by CICO Books
An imprint of Ryland Peters & Small Ltd
20–21 Jockey's Fields 1452 Davis Bugg Road
London WC1R 4BW Warrenton, NC 27589
www.rylandpeters.com
Email: euregulations@rylandpeters.com

10 9 8 7 6 5 4 3 2 1

A CIP record for this book is available from the British Library.
US Library of Congress CIP data has been applied for.

ISBN: 978 1 80065 462 4

Printed in China

Desk editor: Imogen Valler-Miles
Senior designer: Emily Breen
Art director: Sally Powell
Creative director: Leslie Harrington
Production manager: Gordana Simakovic
Head of production: Patricia Harrington
Publishing manager: Carmel Edmonds

The authorised representative in the EEA is
Authorised Rep Compliance Ltd.,
Ground Floor. 71 Lower Baggot Street,
Dublin, D01 P593, Ireland
www.arccompliance.com

SAFETY NOTE

Please note that while the descriptions of the properties of crystals refer to healing benefits, they are not intended to replace diagnosis of illness or ailments, or healing or medicine. Always consult your doctor or other health professional in the case of illness.

Not all crystals are suitable for elixirs. Always check that your chosen crystal's elixir is safe to drink. If you are in doubt, consult your crystal healer.

The safe and proper use of candles and incense is the sole responsibility of the person using them. Do not leave a burning candle unattended. Never burn a candle on or near anything that might catch fire. Keep candles out of the reach of children and pets.

Neither the author nor the publisher can be held responsible for any claim arising out of the use or misuse of suggestions made in this book.

Contents

Introduction

For the past 33 years, I've been exploring the world of crystals, as well as their healing properties and other beneficial effects. However, the story starts way back in time—in fact, around 3.5 million years ago when one of our earliest hominin ancestors picked up a stone and shaped it into a functioning tool—and runs continuously through to today's twenty-first-century Space Age.

Crystals have always been at the cutting edge of human technology. They have helped to guide and shape humanity in all its guises, through all its civilizations, including those which have been recently recorded during the last 8,000 years or so, and those just being rediscovered from prehistory. As well as being described

in ancient texts, such as those from China, Egypt, Greece, India, Israel, and Mesopotamia, physical archaeological evidence has been discovered around the world with finds of crystal and stone tools dating back some 3.5 million years to the very beginnings of our human journey.

Around the world, Indigenous healers, such as shamans and medicine people, have always worked with crystals to help cure the sick and see into other dimensions and times. In fact, just about all the technology used in modern medicine, such as CT scanners and X-ray machines, rely on these same crystals to function and allow doctors to see into the body. Many other modern technologies, including electric vehicles, satellites circling the Earth, interplanetary spacecraft, and even the cell phone in your pocket rely on the ancient power of crystals.

Within the following pages, I take you through humanity's crystal history to today and beyond into the world that we and our children might one day live in. This book challenges our concept of the past and opens doors to the future, but it's not just to be read. With plenty of practical exercises, you will discover how to connect to crystals, your past, and maybe even your future, on a journey through time and through yourself.

I use the term "crystal" colloquially to encompass the whole mineral world, which includes crystals, minerals, stones, rocks, pebbles on a beach, huge megaliths, and potentially even mountains. They are all part of our natural world. In some Native American cultures, crystals are referred to as the Stone People, and they have been helping our technical evolution for millions of years. We live on a crystalline planet which our prehuman ancestors worked to their advantage, slowly bringing humanity to its current place where we are exploring the stars and looking for other crystalline planets that may support life.

Enjoy, experience, and experiment with this book, and follow the stepping stones I offer to understanding our past and our future.

Chapter 1

Cavemen to Astronauts:

History Through the Eyes of Crystals and Minerals

Human development has always depended on the abilities and power of crystals—every civilization throughout history has developed technology or healing practices based on crystals. From early hominins to modern *Homo sapiens*, there is one thing each era has in common—working with crystals to create and form the latest tools of the time. Today, we rely on crystals in our cell phones, computers, lasers, for space travel, and much, much more. Who knows where crystal technology will take us in the future?

Just One Morning...

When you wake up in the morning, what do you do? Perhaps your alarm has gone off on your quartz clock, watch, or cell phone. Then maybe you turn on the light, which is powered by electricity that may come from solar panels on your roof or from an electrical grid, which is powered, at least in part, by crystalline technology.

You cook breakfast in your microwave oven and eat it while watching the television, listening to the radio, or streaming music through your Wi-Fi. Next, you grab some clean clothes from your tumble dryer, put some dirty ones in your washing machine, and turn the dishwasher on.

You hop into your car and drive to work, but there's traffic, so you check your satnav or GPS device for a different route, or maybe you have taken the bus or train instead. Running late, you get to your office, turn on your computer, and then look at the beautiful amethyst crystal sitting on your desk and you feel a calmness come over you. And you realize that every single thing you have done this morning has relied on crystal technology.

Just imagine our ancient ancestors sitting under the stars on a moonlit night and imagining their future...

A Crystal Timeline

Crystals have played a crucial role throughout human history. This timeline highlights some of the most interesting ways in which we have worked with crystals through the ages. Some dates are approximate.

3.5 million years ago, Cradle of Humankind, South Africa

Excavations at the Cradle of Humankind (a site roughly 30 miles (50 km) northwest of Johannesburg, South Africa) have unearthed ancient stone tools that would have been employed by our early human ancestors at this time.

Cave at the Cradle of Humankind, South Africa

3.2 million years ago, Ethiopia

Carnelian beads were placed in burials, presumably to protect the soul on its journey to the afterlife. It was only a short time after our ancestors first started working with crystals and stones as everyday tools that they began to link them with their spiritual beliefs.

Carnelian beads

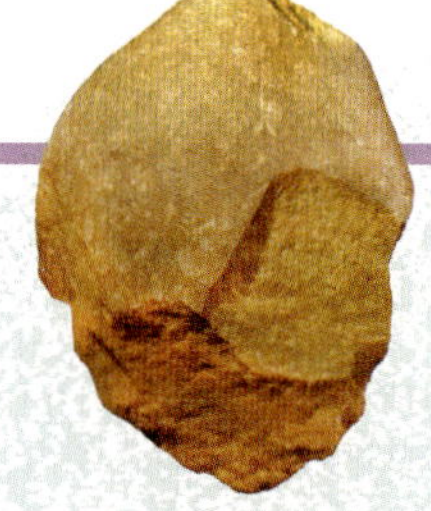

Example of an Oldowan stone tool

2.9 million years ago, Nyayanga, Kenya

Early hominins used stone toolkits (known as Oldowan tools), which included hammerstones (rounded stones used as a hammering tool), cores, and sharp, cutting flakes. Collectively, these tools were used to pound, scrape, and cut both plant and animal material—this included the butchery of hippopotamuses. Recovered from an excavation site called Nyayanga in western Kenya, these ancient tools were much more sophisticated than older stone tools that have been discovered.

2.5–1.9 million years ago, East Africa

It is likely that early humans were experimenting with controlled fire throughout this period.

1.9 million years ago, Turkana Basin (which stretches into Kenya, Ethiopia, South Sudan, and Uganda)

Fossil records suggest that controlled fire was regularly being used for the first time. Ancient hominins would have created fire by striking two pieces of flint or pyrite together to produce a spark, which was then caught in a combustible wad. Fire would have provided light, warmth, safety, and the ability to cook food.

Early hominins used flint (below) to create fire, as well as pyrite.

Fire: A Turning Point in Human History

Up until this point in evolution, like most other animals on the planet, we spent most of our time doing three things: eating, reproducing, and resting.
Then came fire…

- **Light** allowed us to do things for longer. We were no longer limited in our activity by sunlight or the full moon.
- **Warmth** permitted our global expansion by enabling us to live in less hospitable climates, which opened up new areas for exploration.
- **Safety**, brought about by other animals' fear of fire, meant less time focused on defence.
- **Cooking** enabled us to live off less food (because cooked food contains more calories), and spend less time hunting and gathering.

In a short time, in evolutionary terms, we changed physically—our bowel shortened because cooked food is easier to digest, so we could make do with a smaller abdomen, allowing other parts of the body, such as the lungs and the brain, to increase in size. The brain developed and we began to occupy ourselves with art, stories, looking back in time, and contemplating and planning for the future.

The ability to create and control fire was a big game changer in human evolution.

700,000 years ago, Lomekwi 3 Site, West Turkana, Kenya

The next stage of tool development included sharp stone tools, hammers, and anvils, which were utilized by our ancestral cousins and still predate the earliest *Homo* species.

335,000 years ago, Cradle of Humankind, South Africa

There is evidence from the Rising Star cave system at the Cradle of Humankind (see page 11) to suggest that *Homo naledi* (an extinct human relative) buried their dead and made etchings on the cave walls. Stone tools were discovered nearby, which were first used to smooth the rock surface, then to carve the markings.

105,000 years ago, Ga-Mohana Hill North Rockshelter, Kalahari Desert, South Africa

Calcite crystals have been discovered at a sacred shelter in the Kalahari Desert, away from their natural environment. This suggests that the crystals were deliberately collected and transported there from another location for a specific and special purpose.

Kalahari Desert, South Africa

Crystal Practices in the Kalahari Desert

- The crystals were all clear, optical calcite crystals (also called "Iceland spa"), which exhibit double refraction and could be regarded as being quite magical, though they don't have an obvious practical purpose.
- Burned ostrich eggshell fragments and crushed animal bones were also found at the site, which are possible indicators of ritualized feasting or offerings.
- This is an example of early humans displaying complex cultural and symbolic behavior.
- The site has been in perpetual use and is still considered holy by the local people.

100,000 years ago, Lemuria (modern-day Madagascar and India)
Crystals, notably quartz, were possibly employed in technology and in the recording of the Lemurian civilization (see Chapter 3, page 52).

Obsidian arrowhead

74,000 years ago, Ethiopia
Human technology moved on—the bow and arrow were invented, and jasper and obsidian were employed to create arrowheads for this new weapon. Stone arrowheads have also been discovered dating from this period.

40,000 years ago, Japan
There is possible evidence of microlithic tools being used at this time (see also "17,000 years ago," page 16).

Lemurian quartz crystal

Archery was a primary hunting technique in prehistoric times.

33,000 years ago, Chiquihuite Cave, Mexico
Cutting tools made from stone and shaped crystal points have been discovered in a high-altitude cave in the Astillero Mountains in Mexico. Many of the artifacts, specifically human-made tools, show signs of wear from use.

17,000 years ago, Magdalenian Cultures, Europe
Microlithic technology was developed to create composite tools and weapons by joining small, razor-sharp crystal or stone flakes to another structural material, such as bone or wood. This was a major leap in technological advancement because it made much more efficient use of available materials, especially cherts (primarily flint), but it also required great skill in manufacturing the component parts.

9,000 years ago, Mesopotamia (modern-day Iraq, as well as parts of Iran, Syria, and Turkey)
Crystals were considered powerful tools for divination. There are records of rose quartz, chlorite stone, and other materials being employed as amulets for protection and healing. In the earliest known writings from this period, all of these practices were considered normal, which suggests they were not new discoveries and that their origins are much older. Rose quartz beads have also been found dating back to this time. (See also page 106.)

Tunnel entrance to the Chiquihuite Cave in Mexico

Rose quartz and chlorite in quartz

6,500 years ago, Egypt

The ancient Egyptians held a strong belief in the magical powers of crystals and stones, primarily for health and for protection in this life and the next. Chrysolite, peridot, topaz, galena, lapis lazuli, and malachite were all commonly employed in spiritual practices. Many practical, everyday objects were made of crystals, and crystals were worn to demonstrate power and position. This practice continues around the world to this day, with jewels integrated into sacred objects of power, such as the Crown Jewels of the United Kingdom. (See also page 107.)

Peridot

6,000 years ago, Mesopotamia (modern-day Iraq, as well as parts of Iran, Syria, and Turkey)

The Sumerians, an ancient civilization of Mesopotamia, employed crystals in magical formulas for healing. This was possibly the first record of crystal elixirs, which were also utilized in Samaria, an ancient region of Israel, 3,000 years later (see page 108).

5,000 years ago (or longer) to modern day, China

Traditional Chinese Medicine has its roots in Chinese shamanism. Like many shamanic traditions from around the world, crystals were (and still are) worked with extensively in China for healing and divination. Also around this time, chlorite stone and jade were formed into disk beads, ornaments, and practical vessels. (See also page 108.)

The *bi* is a flat, circular jade artifact from ancient China.

5,000 years ago, Israel and Egypt

The Bible mentions minerals, rocks, and crystals more than 1,700 times, along with references to their special powers, healing properties, and energy from God. Sometimes, the Bible also includes crystals and gemstones as metaphors, including "as clear as crystal" (Revelation 22:1) and "salt of the Earth" (Matthew 5:13). Agate was one of the gems set into the breastplate of the High Priest. It was thought to protect him from the all-consuming power of God, allowing him to be in the presence of God, without being consumed by God's energy, and to interpret and relay his words, commands, and teachings to the people.

5,000 years ago, British Isles, France, and Portugal

Giant megalithic stone monuments, including Stonehenge and Avebury stone circles, were built in the UK and other parts of Europe to connect people to the celestial world and to mark special moments in the calendar, such as the summer and winter solstices. Crystals were worn as amulets and worked with for healing, and everyday objects, such as spearheads and knives, have also been unearthed from this period. (See also page 109.)

3,500 years ago to modern day, Mexico and Central and South America

The Olmec, Toltec, Aztec, Maya, and Inca civilizations all employed crystals for both ritualistic purposes and as everyday practical tools and weapons. Some tools were highly decorated with other crystals and minerals, such as gold, jade, and turquoise, with jade being more highly valued than gold. (See also page 108.)

Avebury (below) is the largest stone circle in Britain.

3,000 years ago, Mesopotamia (modern-day Iraq, as well as parts of Iran, Syria, and Turkey)

There is evidence that the Assyrians living in the northern part of the area crafted rose quartz jewelry, which was worn to bring them beauty and love. The Chaldeans, based in southeastern Mesopotamia, were famous for their contributions to mathematics, science, the arts, literature, and governance. They were the first to formalize astronomy with strong links to astrology, and to make connections between planets and gems. This is possibly the first link to the concept of birthstones, where crystals and gems are connected to a time of the year, just as planets have been linked to the seasons and festivals throughout the year. (See also pages 44–49.)

2,300–1,400 years ago, Greece

Crystals and minerals were used extensively in all walks of life in ancient Greece, from the spiritual (amethyst was worn as a sign of power and to protect the wearer from intoxication) to the mundane, including as building materials and decoration for both public buildings and private homes.

On Stones

The Greek philosopher Theophrastus (371–287 BCE) wrote *Peri Lithon* (meaning "On Stones"), which is the basis of today's modern scientific classification of gemstones. He presented a taxonomy of known gems, their origins, physical properties, and magical and healing powers. Although much of this information is still accepted today by the scientific community, the magical and healing properties have been ignored despite having the same historic evidence.

The Parthenon is an ancient Greek temple in Athens, Rome.

1,600 years ago, UK
Amethyst beads were placed in Anglo-Saxon graves across the UK, indicating a strong belief in an afterlife and the power of amethyst to help the soul on its journey.

1890s, India
Scientist Jagadish Chandra Bose employed galena crystals to detect radio signals, which led to the development of crystal wireless radio sets. These radio sets became very popular during the 1920s and continued to be so—in fact, my father made one for me when I was a child!

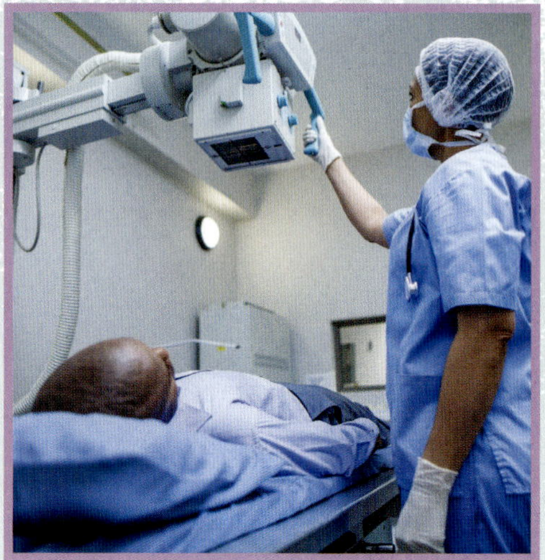
X-ray equipment utilizes various crystals.

1912, Germany
Physicist Max von Laue was the first person to discover X-ray diffraction by sending a beam of X-rays through copper sulfate crystals. Variously sphalerite, diamond, and graphite X-ray machines have been developed. Today, molybdenum is the most common crystal used in X-ray machines.

Crystal wireless set

1915, France
The first practical sonar device to detect submarines was invented by physicist Paul Langevin. Quartz crystals were placed between metal plates with a hydrophone (a device that detects underwater sounds) attached, which returned an echo bouncing off a submarine.

1917, New Jersey, USA
The first crystal oscillator was built using halite at Bell Telephone Laboratories.

1921, Rhode Island, USA
Physicist Walter Guyton Cady developed the first quartz crystal oscillator, which created a stable frequency reference, allowing anyone to tune in to their favorite radio station.

Quartz crystals played a significant role in the development of sonar technology.

1927, Russia

Although LED (light-emitting diode) technology was invented by scientist Oleg Losev in the 1920s, it wasn't commercially available until 1962. LEDs employ natural crystals, such as silicon carbide, gallium nitride, and gallium arsenide, which release photons of light when an electrical current passes through them. Different combinations allow specific wavelengths of light, which we see as colors, to be displayed. Today, LEDs are used in many forms of lighting, as well as in cars, sports stadium floodlights, and cell phones. They are also used in some cancer treatments and in Li-Fi—a data transmission system similar to Wi-Fi but which uses light waves instead of radio waves to carry information.

1954, New Jersey, USA

The first practical solar cell using crystalline silicon was invented at Bell Laboratories. Used to generate power from the Sun's radiation, solar cells have led to the commercial development of today's solar technology (see box below).

LED floodlights are used to illuminate sports stadiums around the world.

Solar Cells

Solar cells are an integral part of zero-emission energy production, which is essential due to the climate changes in our warming world. As well as in commercial solar farms, solar cells can be seen on many buildings around the world, both commercial and domestic, producing localized energy. But the truly amazing application of solar cells is that they have been a key part of space programs since the 1950s, producing the power to run not only the International Space Station but also many of NASA's spacecraft, including the Parker Solar Probe and the James Webb Space Telescope.

1960, California, USA

Physicist Theodore Maiman developed the first laser at Hughes Research Laboratories. This laser employed a ruby crystal to generate laser light. Ruby lasers produce a red light, while blue and green lasers employ sapphire and alexandrite, respectively.

1964, New Jersey, USA

LCD (liquid crystal display) was invented at RCA Laboratories following earlier research in the 1880s, which had identified liquid crystals in carrot cholesterol! George Heilmeier developed the research into the practical LCD that is now used in smartphones, televisions, computer monitors, in-car displays, and medical equipment.

Barcode scanners are one of many practical applications of laser light.

The invention of LCD technology transformed the development of technical devices.

Ruby

1967, Switzerland and Japan

Although the first quartz clock was invented in 1927 in the USA, it was four decades later that both the Japanese company Seiko and the Centre Electronique Horloger in Switzerland almost simultaneously produced the first quartz crystal watches. Quartz watches are essential time-keeping devices for billions of people every day and quartz clocks also appear in lots of other technology that we rely on to keep time in the twenty-first century, such as computers, smartphones, and ovens.

2012, Japan

Tech company Hitachi unveiled a quartz crystal computer storage chip the size of a thumbnail that can hold 300 TB of information. It is able to endure extreme temperatures—it has been frozen as well as heated to temperatures of 1,832°F (1,000°C) with no loss of data. Hitachi claim that the chip may hold data for 100 million years with no degradation. It's said that diamonds are forever, but maybe quartz crystals are, too! (See also page 54.)

Billions of people around the world rely on their quartz crystal watch every day.

Himalayan quartz crystal

Today and in the Future...

Crystals are found in cell phones, computers, GPS devices, electric vehicles (EVs), spacecraft, washing machines, tumble dryers, microwave ovens, stoves, electric barbecues, inkjet printers, X-ray machines, CT scanners, microscopes, high-quality lenses in telescopes, high-quality camera and optical equipment, sound recording and playback equipment, lighting, lasers, and much, much more. Our twenty-first-century lifestyle would not exist without crystal technology.

Crystals are grown on the International Space Station!

It is normal to find defects in almost all natural crystals growing on Earth, which can negatively impact the quality of the crystal and be detrimental to the properties that scientists want to harness. But NASA is growing natural crystals on the International Space Station! Growing crystals in space allows for perfect growth conditions, which are unchallenged by the Earth's natural environment.

Diamond crystals are being used to build quantum computers (an emerging technology based on the properties of quantum mechanics). This is predicted to change both personal computing and the power of the internet. It has the potential to solve complex problems that are beyond the capabilites of conventional computers. This could lead to more accurate severe weather forecasting, improved detection of early cancers in healthcare scans, and more efficient use of transport services.

DID YOU KNOW?

Modern cell phones contain more than 40 crystals and minerals. They are found in the screen, the battery, the display and back lighting, the electrical circuitry, the casing, the microphone, the speakers, vibration alerts, and the camera.

Single-crystal electrodes are being developed for electric vehicles (EVs) which could extend the lifespan of EV batteries to millions of miles. Research into regenerative medicine has demonstrated that crystals have the ability to promote tissue regeneration by attracting unspecialized cells to the affected area and encouraging them to differentiate to the desired tissue type.

Crystals are utilized in batteries for electric vehicles.

Time crystals were originally theorized by theoretical physicist Frank Wilczek in 2012 and they were first created in 2016 at the University of Maryland, USA. In an ordinary crystal, atoms are arranged in a repeating three-dimensional pattern in space, but the atoms in time crystals are arranged in patterns that repeat in time. As a result, time crystals have amazing potential! Their back-and-forth movement in time gives them the ability to produce continuous "free" energy. The shifting state of their molecules through time poses the possibility of time crystals perhaps leading to the opportunity for time travel.

And if you believe that some of this sounds like science fiction, just think about our ancient ancestors sitting under the stars on a moonlit night, discussing how if only they could control fire, it would change the world...

PRACTICAL EXERCISE:
CREATE YOUR OWN CRYSTAL TIMELINE

Making a personal crystal timeline is a great way to document your thoughts and feeling about your crystals, and the impact they have had on your life. You can do this by yourself or with friends. You will need a blank piece of paper and a pen.

1. Think back to the first crystal you can remember in your life. Maybe you were given it as a child or picked a stone up on a beach. Perhaps it came from a museum gift store, or was in a piece of jewelry. Write down the name of the crystal, or just its color if you don't know its name.
2. Think about this crystal and any details you can remember about it. For example, why did you like it at the time? Who bought it for you and how did you feel about them? Do you still feel the same way now? Has the crystal helped you through difficult times? Does it remind you of a relationship? Add all these thoughts and feelings to your timeline.
3. You might have memories about a few or even many more crystals. Repeat the above process for each one.
4. When you have finished, choose some other crystals from your collection that you feel drawn to right now. Follow the same process as above, but this time, focus on the crystal rather than the memory. Some of these may be crystals you've already documented from past memories, and it's fine to add this new information to what you have already recorded.
5. You can add as many crystals as you like to your timeline; it is not fixed, and you can continue to add more in the future too. Your feelings and memories might change with time, so you can add more information whenever you like. Don't remove anything, even if it brings up uncomfortable feelings, because all of your thoughts are part of your experience.
6. When you have finished, read through the crystal timeline you have created. There will be some thoughts that inspire you and give you strength and confidence, and some that may be challenging. If this exercise has brought up any difficult thoughts for you, speak to a friend or family member or seek professional support.

Chapter 2

Crystal Legends:
Stories from Around the World

The word "crystal" comes from the Greek word *krýstallos*, which is derived from *krýos*, meaning "icy cold." The ancient Greeks believed that quartz crystals were ice frozen so hard by their gods that it would never thaw. Other stories about crystals abound throughout the world and all ages of history. These tales often speak of the powers of crystals and how they "saved the day"; some reference their properties, such as being "as clear as a diamond" or "as strong as a rock"; while others provide us with messages. This chapter includes some of my favorite crystal legends to throw light on the tales of the past.

Opal

Forming masses, opal occurs in a multitude of colors, including pink, black, beige, blue, yellow, brown, orange, red, green, and purple. It can boost creativity, inspiration, and imagination.

Opal sometimes shows "fire" (iridescence) in various colors, which is caused by the diffraction of light within the crystalline structure. This crystal can strengthen psychic abilities, shamanic visions, and memory. It can also remove inhibition and promote both positive and negative characteristics, allowing you to build on good qualities and deal with the bad.

Many cultures suggest a connection between the creation of opal and atmospheric conditions. According to one ancient belief, the storm god —known by different names in various cultures, such as Zeus (ancient Greek), Thor (Norse), Indra (Hindu), and Chaac (Mayan)—was so enraged at the rainbow for ending his storm that he broke it into a thousand tiny pieces. The pieces fell to Earth and became embedded in the rocks, creating a variety of opal called fire opal. Stories from Arabian folklore suggest that opals fell from the sky when very large bolts of lightning flashed in the heavens.

The word "opal" is thought to come from the Latin *opalus* and the Sanskrit *upala*, which means "precious stone." The ancient Greeks attributed opal as a gem of the gods and in ancient Rome, opal was considered a gem of hope. It was believed that opal could prevent despondency and disease, and provide protection against lightning strikes—connecting it full circle back to the story of the storm god.

In the Middle Ages, opals were reputed to cure eye diseases. Wrapped in a bay leaf, an opal was thought to improve the sight of its owner and weaken the sight of others, making the owner invisible. For this attribute, opal was called *patronus furum* (patron of thieves).

The Stone of Invisibility

Invisibility is a funny thing. It has been recorded throughout history to be pure imagination and we have no scientific way of proving it. However, many years ago, I bought my then wife a birthday gift from Brazil of what would have been the largest citrine geode in the UK at that time. International shipping dates back then were unreliable, so I ordered it well in advance to make sure it was here for the day. It arrived a week early. Where to put a wooden shipping crate measuring about 4 ft (120 cm) long, 2 ft (60 cm) tall, and 3 ft (90 cm) wide, I wondered.

At the time, I owned a small crystal store with a room out back for tarot readers. So, I replaced the customers' chairs with the shipping crate, placed a couple of cushions on top, and a small blue opal underneath one of the cushions. The psychic readers all noticed something odd—a shipping crate in their room—but none of their clients saw it. In fact, my wife even had a tarot reading just before her birthday, sat on the crate for about an hour, and didn't see it! So yes, opal is genuinely the stone of invisibility!

Unlucky Opal

By the fourteenth century, opal had become a popular stone for jewelry in Europe. However, its popularity soon waned, with several stories linking opals to misfortune. In the mid-1300s, Europe was devastated by the Black Death, a plague pandemic that killed roughly half the population. People noticed that opals became brilliant when worn by someone who caught the plague, then lost their luster upon the person's death, and so opals became associated with death. This can happen because opals are hydrated (contain water in their crystalline structure), so can be affected by biochemical changes in the skin when they are worn next to it.

It is said that King Louis XIV of France (1638–1715) traveled in coaches named after gemstones. Supposedly, the driver of "Opal" was usually inebriated and had many accidents, and so "Opal" became an unlucky coach to travel in.

In the nineteenth century, Sir Walter Scott's novel *Anne of Geierstein* (1829) featured an enchanted princess, Hermione, who wore an opal in her hair. The opal would change color with her mood, but when a few drops of holy water touched the gem, the princess died. It is thought that Scott was, in fact, referencing Mexican opal, which is a common name for girasol, a variety of quartz. Nevertheless, the story had a powerful influence over superstitious people and significantly impacted the popularity of the gem.

Girasol is a type of clear quartz, sometimes called Mexican opal.

DID YOU KNOW?

Emperor Napoleon famously gifted a stunning black opal (named the "Burning of Troy" due to the flashes of red in the gem) to his wife, Josephine. The crystal subsequently went missing following her death in 1814.

Throughout some periods of history, opals were associated with bad luck, but have now increased in popularity.

Another story that fueled the superstition in the latter part of the nineteenth century was that of the "Grand Opal of Spain." This was a magnificent opal ring gifted to the Spanish King Alfonso XII by his former lover, the Countess of Castiglione, upon his wedding. The new Queen Mercedes took a fancy to this stunning gem and asked her husband to grace her finger with it. A few months later, she died of a mysterious illness. Alfonso gave the ring to his grandmother, then to his sister, and finally to his sister-in-law, who were all in turn carried off by the same mysterious illness! The King then wore the ring himself and soon after, the same illness ended his life too.

Cholera was raging throughout Spain at this time, and was the most likely cause of these royal deaths. Opal had gained a reputation as a protector against cholera, which could explain why the poor King kept gifting the ring to his family members. However, the revengeful Countess had reversed the opal's effect (by means not recorded) to "attract" cholera to his loved ones. This is an example of crystals "working," although not for healing in this case!

Despite its poor reputation, the British Queen Victoria, who reigned from 1837 to 1901, was known to love opals, perhaps because of their healing and protective powers. Her royal endorsement reignited the popularity of opals in Europe.

Ruby

A red variety of corundum in the form of tabular crystals, ruby is associated with knowledge and self-cultivation; it will kick your mind into gear when you feel stuck.

Ruby can help you with new beginnings, creativity, making decisions or changes, financial realism, and finding answers to questions about love and relationships. It brings abundance and helps you to share this from your heart. Ruby also protects from nightmares, relieves anguish, distress, and suffering, helps with distant healing, and strengthens connections with spirit guides (see page 86).

There is an ancient legend from Burma (now Myanmar) that tells of the creation of rubies. It speaks of a giant eagle soaring over a valley looking for food. As the eagle glided high in the sky, it noticed some bright red meat below on the valley floor. The eagle swooped down and attempted to seize the meat but was unable to move it. The eagle tried again and again, each time swooping down and attempting to grasp the meat without success. Finally, the eagle stopped and settled on the valley floor for a closer look. The eagle then realized that the bright red "meat" was not a piece of meat at all—in fact, it was a sacred stone created from the fire and blood of the Earth itself. As the eagle approached with reverence, it was then able to take the stone, which was thought to be the first ruby.

This story is said to have taken place in Mogok, sometimes referred to as the "Valley of Rubies." The Mogok Stone Tract, located in the Kathe District of Upper Myanmar, has been a major source of gemstones for centuries and is particularly well known for its rubies.

Turquoise

This blue, green, or blue-green stone helps you to see the beauty in everything. It forms as masses, crusts, and (rarely) small, short prismatic crystals.

Turquoise brings the mental and spiritual clarity to see your own path. It improves confidence and courage, and helps you to express your truth and be open to communication. It also brings peace of mind.

This stone holds a special significance in some Native American cultures. Indigenous peoples of the American Southwest, such as the Navajo, Apache, and Pueblo, have been employing turquoise in jewelry, trade, and for ceremonial purposes for thousands of years. Referred to as the "stone of life," turquoise is considered to be a stone of blessings, good fortune, protection, and good health. It is symbolic because it signifies life. The sky and water can be seen in its blue-green color, while its brown veins embody the earth—it is the world represented in a stone.

One Navajo story tells of the goddess Estsanatlehi, also known as the "Changing Woman," who appeared as a turquoise woman. Her name refers to the way in which turquoise can change color depending on its environment, such as humidity levels, light exposure, and skin contact, leading some people to consider the stone to be "alive." Another Navajo tale describes how people would dance and cry with joy when it finally rained after a long drought. Their tears mixed with the rain and formed turquoise, giving it another name—the "fallen sky stone."

Turquoise can represent the sky, water, and earth.

Amethyst

This calming crystal is the violet variety of quartz, found as crystals or masses. Its classic purple color is due to manganese and iron inclusions.

Amethyst brings overall protection, and physical, emotional, and mental balance. It can support you when coping with responsibility or stresses and also help to ease grief, homesickness, and insomnia.

The name "amethyst" comes from the Greek word *amethystos*, which translates to "not intoxicated," and originates from an ancient Greek myth. The legend tells of a beautiful young maiden named Amethystos, who was pursued by Dionysus (the god of wine and festivity). Wishing to save her virtue, Amethystos sought help from Artemis (the goddess of innocence and hunting), who transformed Amethystos into a giant, pure quartz statue to protect her from Dionysus. Upon seeing the statue and realizing the consequences of his actions, Dionysus wept remorseful tears of wine over the statue, staining the quartz a deep violet color, thereby creating amethyst.

The Romans inherited the same story (with Dionysus and Artemis replaced with Bacchus and Diana, respectively) and this reinforced the belief that amethyst symbolizes both the influence of intoxication and the strength of abstinence and purity. Amethyst can represent both the wild, intoxicating nature of Dionysus, as well as Artemis's pure nature in the same crystal—it is a realization and expression of duality, of yin and yang, and the balance between them, which we need for a healthy lifestyle.

Dionysus was the Greek god of wine and festivity.

Labradorite

Typically gray-green, pale green, blue, gray-white, or colorless, this feldspar mineral forms as masses and displays visually striking flashes of color. It enables you to see many possibilities at once.

When light enters the surface layers of labradorite, it bounces around in the internal crystalline structure and reflects out from different levels. This optical effect is known as labradorescence. The flashes of color can include blues, greens, oranges, yellows, reds, and violets, and have fascinated people for millennia. Labradorite helps to relieve stress and anxiety, brings clarity of mind, can enable you to see into the future, and allows magic to happen around you, without you really trying. It helps you to find your place in the world.

Labradorite is said to have been "discovered" by Moravian missionaries in 1770, in Labrador, Canada, from which the name is derived. But the Innu and Inuit peoples (distinct Indigenous groups living in parts of Quebec and Newfoundland and Labrador in eastern Canada) already knew of, and had a deep relationship with, labradorite long before then. The Innu people traditionally lived inland whereas the Inuit were coastal dwellers, and because there is labradorite under the land throughout the whole area, a commonly held appreciation of its magical properties and importance within the cultures was accepted. Both the Innu and Inuit peoples of eastern Canada call labradorite the "fire stone" because of its beautiful color show and resemblance to the Northern Lights, also known as aurora borealis.

One story about labradorite tells of a powerful Inuit warrior who saw the amazing array of colors inside the crystals and thought the lights of the aurora borealis were trapped within the rocks! So he hit the labradorite with his spear to free the lights to return to the heavens where they belonged. Some of the light went up to the sky and some stayed inside the labradorite stones.

The Innu have a similar story about labradorite. In their rendition, the star people that live beyond the aurora borealis once actually lived here on Earth inside labradorite. An Innu warrior with a giant hammer delivered a huge blow to the stones, which released most of the stars back to the heavens, but the stars that stayed on Earth remained in the stones of Labrador. This belief echoes astronomical tales from around the world, in which the star people came and then left Earth, leaving behind knowledge, wisdom, and beauty.

Innu shamans work with labradorite to heal a variety of ailments such as stomach and eye problems. Practices include grinding the crystal into a powder and applying it to the body and taping labradorite onto warts to treat them. The Innu people also cut and polish the stones to make jewelry for protection from the spiritual realm, which is unseen but always present.

The brilliant display of colors exhibited by labradorite is reminiscent of the Northern Lights.

Rose Quartz

Forming as pink, crystalline masses and occasionally as rare, small, hexagonal crystals, rose quartz has long been valued for its ability to enhance beauty and to promote love.

In ancient Egypt and ancient Rome, rose quartz was revered for its rejuvenating properties and was thought to promote clear, youthful-looking skin—rose quartz face masks have been discovered in ancient Egyptian tombs. Ancient Chinese practices also employed rose quartz for healing purposes, and the tradition of rubbing rose quartz around the eyes and cheeks in the form of a facial roller or *gua sha* tool continues to this very day.

With its soft, delicate pink hues, and calm, soothing energy, rose quartz is a crystal of the heart and is thought to have been offered as a token of love as early as 600 BCE. Rose quartz promotes close, lasting friendships and encourages romance, love, and intimacy, which makes it a meaningful gift for lovers.

Greek mythology abounds with tales of love, lust, passion, and despair. One story tells of Eros—the god of desire, attraction, and love—and how he brought

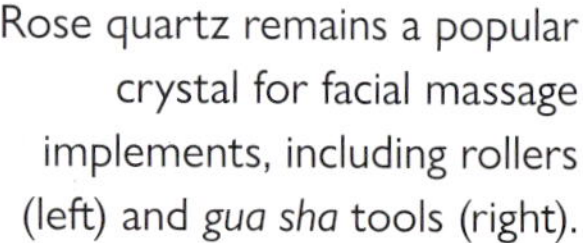

Rose quartz remains a popular crystal for facial massage implements, including rollers (left) and *gua sha* tools (right).

Rose quartz carries the message of unconditional love.

a pink rose quartz down from the heavens to Mount Olympus (the earthly home of the gods) to spread happiness and love in the mortal world.

Another tale speaks of Adonis, who was the mortal lover of Aphrodite—the goddess of love and beauty. One day, Adonis, an accomplished hunter, entered a forest to hunt, despite Aphrodite's pleas for him to give up such a dangerous sport. Aphrodite's jealous ex-lover, Ares, the god of war, saw his chance to seek revenge upon Adonis for taking Aphrodite from him. Ares transformed into a wild boar and attacked Adonis, fatally wounding him. Hearing Adonis's screams, Aphrodite rushed to save him, tearing her clothes and flesh on a thorny briar bush. It is said that the blood from Aphrodite and Adonis mixed and fell onto a nearby quartz crystal, turning it pink. Zeus, king of the gods, seeing the sorrow of lost love, took pity on the torn lovers and declared that he would bring Adonis back to Aphrodite for six months of every year. The bloodstained quartz bloomed into the beauty of rose quartz, which became a symbol of the love shared, lost, and then renewed by Zeus.

PRACTICAL EXERCISE:

CREATE YOUR OWN CRYSTAL LEGEND

Every crystal has a story to tell. This exercise will help you to get to know a crystal by exploring its past. You will need a pen and paper, or a mobile device, to record your experiences. You may want to create a relaxing or mysterious atmosphere by dimming the lights, lighting a candle, and playing some suitable music.

1 Look at your selection of crystals and choose one that you feel drawn to. It could be a crystal that holds special meaning for you or it might be one that sparkles when you look at it.

2 Find a calm, quiet place where you can focus on your crystal undisturbed. Hold your crystal or place it next to you if it's too big or you just don't fancy holding it.

3 Make yourself comfortable, breathe slowly and deeply, and allow yourself to relax while you look at the crystal.

4 Keep your focus on the crystal, and, after a little while, it will start to take you on a journey into its past. This crystal has likely been around for millions or even hundreds of millions of years. It has more knowledge than you can imagine!

5 As you breathe, let your inner mind explore the crystal's energy. Close your eyes and imagine a golden cord from your third eye (the middle of your mind) connecting you to the crystal's energy center.

6 Notice what you can see, feel, hear, smell, and taste through this golden cord that is connecting you to the crystal. Don't restrain your imagination, let it flow…

7 When you feel ready, open your eyes and start writing down your experiences. Even if you just have feelings, record these. As you begin to write, you will recall more and more detail. You will have listened to the crystal and heard its story.

If you like, you can repeat this with all your crystals, one at a time.

Crystal Associations

Different cultures throughout history have linked stones to planets, months, seasons, and the Zodiac. The associated gemstones vary depending on beliefs, the area of the world, and the availability of natural materials in different regions of the Earth. There are also crystals that tie in with day and night, times of the day, and days of the week. All of these are good, valid reasons for selecting a crystal.

Crystals Associated With Months of the Year

The idea of a link between specific crystals and calendar dates comes from biblical times. Both Josephus (a first-century Jewish historian) and Saint Jerome (who translated the Bible into Latin in the late fourth century) commented on the following connections between the 12 stones in the High Priest's breastplate and the 12 months of the year.

Crystals Associated With the Seasons

In sixteenth-century Europe, it became fashionable to carry or wear particular crystals that represented each of the four seasons in the Northern Hemisphere. Emerald is the crystal for spring, its green color symbolizing growth and sensitivity, new beginnings, and new birth. Emerald also represents Venus, the Roman goddess of love, and is therefore an appropriate crystal because spring is regarded as the season of love. Ruby, the "King of Jewels," is the crystal for summer. Its red color symbolizes the fire of the Sun and it represents expression and creativity. Autumn is associated with sapphire, which is a stone for clarity and insight. This season may be a sad time for some because the summer is over, leaves fall from the trees, and life generally slows down in preparation for the dark winter ahead. Sapphire helps to protect against depression and supports you in looking forward to the next spring. Diamond is appropriate for winter because it is the hardest, coldest, brightest gem, and it often reminds us of ice.

Crystals by Birth Date (Birthstones)

Astrologers believe that when you are born, your body has a natural vibration linked to the Universe, of which you are a part. If this vibration can be recreated around you all the time, then everything in your life will flow better. Your zodiac (Sun) sign is determined by the position of the Sun in relation to the Earth at your time of birth. Dates change slightly because our calendar doesn't exactly match the Earth's orbit around the Sun.

If you are born on the cusp of two zodiac signs, check an ephemeris (see page 138) for exact times and dates. If you require accuracy in this matter, refer to a professional astrologer.

Agate is the birthstone for Gemini. This photo shows drusy black agate.

Carrying or wearing your birthstone helps to replicate the vibrations of the stars and planets at your time of birth. These will be drawn down toward you, boosting your aura (see page 115). This is protective physically, emotionally, mentally, and spiritually. It is also thought that such birthstones will increase your body's own healing power. You will have more energy, recover quicker from illness and injury, and feel stronger emotionally and mentally to cope with stress.

Your birthstone shouldn't restrict you in your choice of crystals. If you feel drawn to a specific crystal, it will benefit you even if you don't know how or why. There are many different birthstones for each zodiac sign, and often one crystal is linked to several signs. The chart shown opposite provides a typical, but not definitive, selection.

It wasn't until the eighteenth century, in Poland, that it became popular to carry birthstones, and this tradition then rapidly spread throughout Europe and the rest of the Western world. Prior to this, gemstones and crystals were usually worn or carried for their healing benefits.

Zodiac Sign	Dates	Crystal
Aries	March 21–April 20	Bloodstone
Taurus	April 21–May 21	Jade
Gemini	May 22–June 21	Agate
Cancer	June 22–July 23	Moonstone
Leo	July 24–August 23	Jasper
Virgo	August 24–September 23	Carnelian
Libra	September 24–October 23	Rose quartz
Scorpio	October 24–November 22	Unakite
Sagittarius	November 23–December 21	Obsidian
Capricorn	December 22–January 20	Tiger's eye
Aquarius	January 21–February 19	Quartz
Pisces	February 20–March 20	Amethyst

Crystals Associated With the Planets

The Chaldeans—who lived in Mesopotamia around 4000 BCE and were famous for studying the stars to foretell the future—recorded connections between the seven classical planets, including the Sun and the Moon, and gemstones (see chart opposite). The Zodiac had been observed by ancient astronomers and stargazers, and it is very probable that similar connections would have been made by the Chaldeans. The outer planets Neptune and Uranus, and other planetary bodies such as Pluto, weren't discovered until later.

Other cultures have suggested different connections between crystals and planetary bodies. For example, in Hindu tradition, topaz is connected to Jupiter, coral to Mars, emerald to Mercury, sapphire to Saturn, diamond to Venus, and ruby to the Sun. Native American and Chinese cultures also have their own traditions, which do not correspond to the connections made by the Chaldeans. The ancient Egyptians referred extensively to both their own version of the Zodiac and different crystals, although the details are difficult to follow as they used different constellations to those in the modern day. However, this is in part why there is so much confusion surrounding contemporary birthstones; for this reason, I often suggest several correspondences between the Zodiac and crystals in my books.

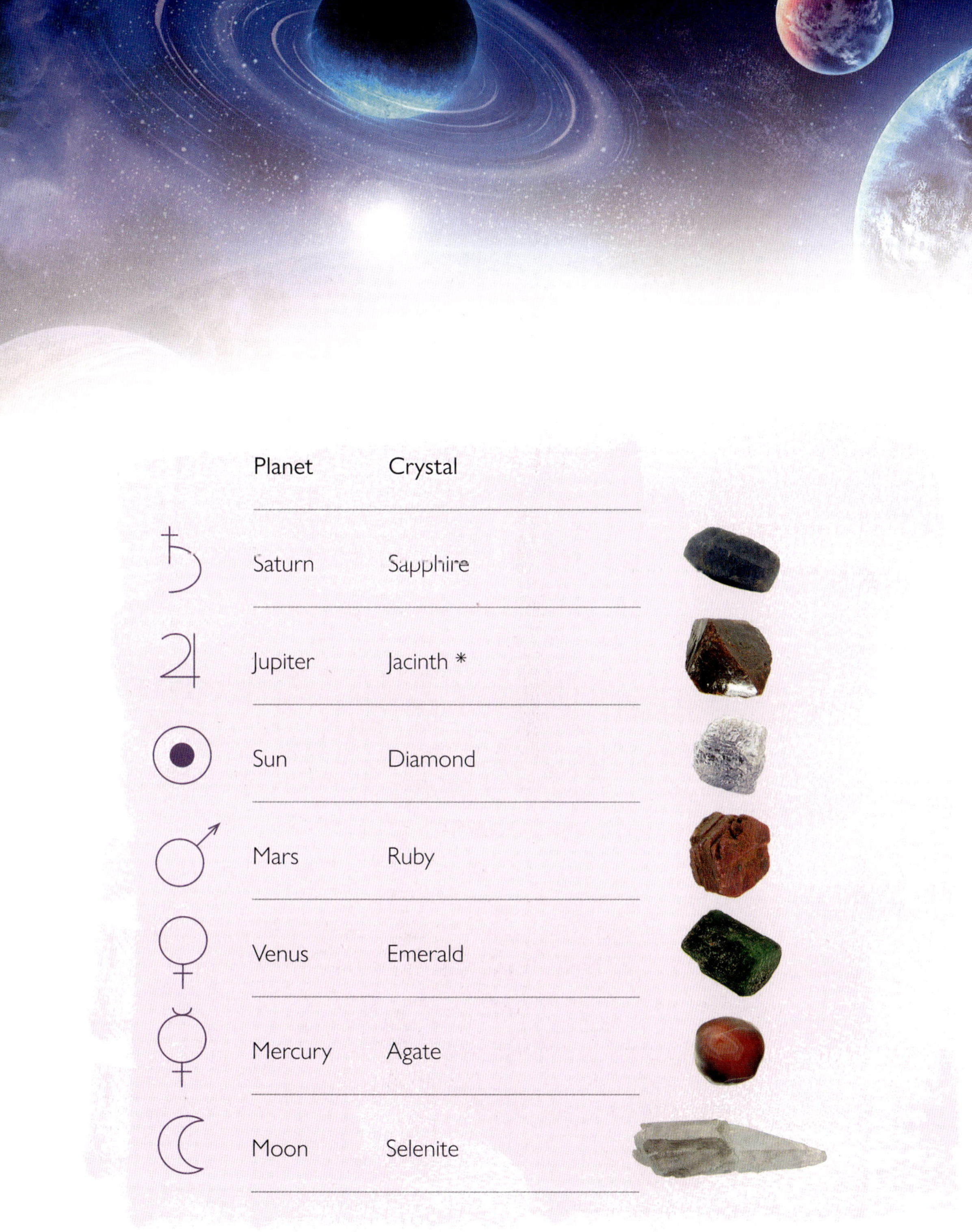

Planet	Crystal
Saturn	Sapphire
Jupiter	Jacinth *
Sun	Diamond
Mars	Ruby
Venus	Emerald
Mercury	Agate
Moon	Selenite

* *Now known as hyacinth, a brilliant red zircon*

Chapter 3

Lemurian Quartz Crystals:

How They Became Supercharged Healers

According to legend, Lemurian civilization was a highly advanced ancient society that predated Atlantis. Priests of Lemuria are believed to have worked extensively with crystals, especially quartz crystals. The priests predicted the catastrophic destruction of their civilization long before it happened, allowing them to program the quartz crystals with the knowledge of their society, which they then sealed in caves to protect them until the time was right for rediscovery.

Lemuria

Lemuria is the name of a lost, low-lying landmass in the Indian Ocean, the remnants of which are present-day Madagascar and India. The Lemurian civilization has been speculated about since Victorian times.

The word "Lemuria" comes from the word "lemur," which is the name of a small primate that inhabits Madagascar. Lemurs were named in 1758 by Swedish biologist Carl Linnaeus who derived the name from the Latin word *lemures* (which means "spirits of the night"), due to the nocturnal nature of these animals.

In the mid-nineteenth century, zoologists pondered why lemur fossils had been found on Madagascar as well as in India, which is some 3,350 miles (about 5,400 km) away across the ocean. Since lemurs cannot swim or fly, in 1864, the English zoologist Philip Sclater proposed that a land bridge must have connected the two areas in the past. This is strongly supported by the crystals of these regions, too, because identical ruby and sapphire deposits exist in these areas. Sclater named this theoretical landmass Lemuria and it has since become associated with many spiritual and metaphysical ideas.

The subcontinent we know today as India was once an island. It was moving toward and eventually crashed into Asia around 50 million years ago, pushing up the Himalayas and the Tibetan Plateau. Madagascar was part of this moving island continent. Sclater had been correct—there had indeed been a physical land connection between India and Madagascar. The Indian island continent continued on its journey north into Asia for millions of years until about 12,900 years ago—the time of the Younger Dryas cataclysm.

Lemuria is named after the lemur.

Lemuria was part of the Indian island continent that collided with Asia around 50 million years ago and pushed up the Himalayas.

The Younger Dryas was a period of extreme and rapid cooling of the Earth's climate. This resulted in the extinction of megafauna (large mammals), such as mammoths, as well as the destruction of civilizations and the decimation of the human population. This cataclysm destroyed the Lemurian civilization. But unlike the destruction of other ancient civilizations that have come and gone, this was not a sudden, destructive event, such as a tsunami, volcanic eruption, war, or flood. Indeed, the wise men and women—I wonder what they called them; perhaps shamans, priests, seers, prophets—of Lemuria would have predicted the end of their civilization eventually happening for many years, possibly even for generations, even if the Younger Dryas wasn't the expected ending. This allowed the Lemurians to program crystals with all their knowledge and seed the information for future generations to find all over their known world.

No one is certain how the Lemurians programmed crystals with knowledge, but it was probably through focusing the mind and applying pressure to the crystals. Maybe they even selected crystals from the Himalayas—which would have experienced the great natural pressure created by the India–Asia collision—to enhance the process. Maybe they were creating the first memory seeds or silicon chips, like the ones we use today.

Lemurian quartz crystals carry ancient knowledge and wisdom.

Sounds implausible? Well, one of the earliest computer memory devices employed quartz crystals to both generate and detect sound pulses traveling through tubes filled with mercury, which are known as mercury delay lines. And then there's today… with the Japanese tech conglomerate Hitachi employing quartz crystals to hold massive amounts of data—up to 300 TB—by applying the binary computer code (which uses only two digits, 0 and 1) to the same part of the crystal at different pressures.

Due to the distribution of Lemurian crystals in the Ural Mountains in Russia, Minas Gerais in Brazil, and the Santander Department in Colombia (some people also suggest that Lemurian crystals are found in Tibet and Zambia) we must consider that there were several advanced civilizations coexisting in different areas around the world, which had similar crystal technology and knowledge (see box opposite). However the physical end came to Lemuria and other pre-Younger Dryas cultures, we have been left with some amazingly powerful and wise quartz healing crystals.

Other Lost Civilizations?

Several other civilizations may have existed at the same time as Lemuria, such as Mu (the remnants of which are possibly the Hawaiian archipelago in the Pacific Ocean) and Atlantis (likely the modern-day Canary Islands in the Atlantic Ocean). There is also strong evidence of a civilization existing in Japan prior to the Younger Dryas, which was responsible for the creation of stone tools, pottery, massive stone-built sacred sites, permanent settlements, and burial places. This civilization also produced clay figures, called *dogu*, with ritualistic purposes linked to their spiritual beliefs. The development of this society seemed to have stalled for 10,000 years around the time of the Younger Dryas before "new" technology, such as wet-rice agriculture and metalwork, was brought from the Asian mainland around 300 BCE. The ancient underwater site of the Yonaguni Monument, which became covered as sea levels rose at the end of the Younger Dryas, could be the telltale sign of an even earlier Japanese civilization.

The lost continent of Mu may have been destroyed by a volcanic eruption.

Lemurian Quartz Crystals

These crystals allow connection to the wisdom of ancient civilizations and are regarded by crystal healers as the most powerful of the healing quartzes.

All quartz crystals channel any energy, but the Lemurian varieties do this exceptionally well and can help with any condition. They are specifically helpful for acute pain relief and any form of physical discomfort. Lemurian quartz crystals boost vivacity, open the heart, dispel negativity, and improve the quality of life. They've been called "all singing, all dancing" crystals because they make you feel happier and reenergize your zest for life in all situations. They can also help you focus your mind, especially during meditation. On a healing level, all clear quartz Lemurian crystals are connected to all the chakras (see page 118) and are also associated with all astrological star signs (see page 47).

Lemurian quartz crystal

Identifying Lemurian Quartz Crystals

It can be difficult to identify Lemurian quartz crystals without feeling their energy (which always feels different to other quartz crystals), but here are some pointers to help you.

- Lemurian quartz crystals are clear, hexagonal crystals with small terminations and horizontal striations (ridges or "barcodes") on either all six sides or three alternate sides. You can physically feel these when you rub your thumb up and down the crystal. Specifically, Lemurian seed crystals have alternating sides exhibiting these striations and flatness with brilliant clarity.

- There will be a brilliance within the crystal. The outside might range from translucent to transparent, and could be frosted, but they are always brilliantly bright on the inside.
- These crystals focus light very well (see page 122).
- They make parts of your body feel physically different. People who are sensitive to crystal energies (see tip box below) feel something different when holding a Lemurian crystal. I always feel an energy, like a warmth, coming from my shoulders, up the back of my neck, and into my head. Other people feel different sensations, often in their hands and arms, heart, or head.
- Lemurian crystals have so far only been found in parts of Colombia, Russia, and Brazil (see page 54).

Remember that natural crystals will exhibit variations, so not all Lemurian quartzes will display all of these properties clearly. It is also worth noting that crystals from other areas may display some of these characteristics without being Lemurian crystals, so it is always best to ask the crystal store or supplier to verify exactly where the crystal comes from when you buy it. For example, some of the amazing quartz crystals from Mount Ida near Little Rock, Arkansas, USA, often exhibit most or all of the Lemurian traits but feel very different energetically because they are not Lemurian crystals.

TIP

If you don't think you are sensitive to crystal energies, try shaking your hands very vigorously for a couple of minutes before holding your crystal. This will make your hands more receptive to any energy work.

Varieties of Lemurian Quartz Crystals

Here are some of the varieties of Lemurian quartz crystals that I work with. I encourage you to try the practical exercises in order to experience the powerful healing properties of these crystals for yourself.

Colombian Lemurian Quartz Crystal

Aptly named "blades of light," Colombian Lemurian quartz crystals are some of the clearest and brightest quartz crystals I have seen. They come from the Santander Department in the central-northern part of Colombia. These crystals are excellent tools for self-development, meditation, and connecting to your own past. You might see them referred to as "Lemurian clear quartz," "Lemurian rock crystal," and "Lemurian crystal," but these names can also be applied to other varieties of Lemurian quartz crystals.

Blue Mist Variety (Colombia)

Every now and again, I come across a new type of crystal that says "Wow!" It jumps up and down, waves, shouts, sings, and throws a bucket of cold water in my face! Then it lets me gently bathe and relax in its glorious crystal light. Blue mist Lemurian quartz crystal (also called blue smoke Lemurian quartz crystal) from Colombia is one such crystal.

Technically, it is a clear quartz crystal with internal faulting and microscopic inclusions of the mineral cookeite, which creates the misty inner appearance. There are often yellow-brown colors near the base of the crystal due to the presence of another mineral, limonite.

Blue mist Colombian Lemurian quartz crystal

As a crystal healer, I believe that blue mist Colombian Lemurian quartz crystals have the following qualities:

- They make you feel like a young child and an old wise person at the same time.
- These crystals help you to explore your spiritual world while keeping you grounded in the physical one, allowing you to discover your inner self and release trapped emotions and emotional pain from the past, such as childhood or relationship issues, and to explore past lives (see also pages 76–85).
- They smell musky at the limonite base, while the clear point smells like fresh mountain air. Try smelling your crystals if you haven't before! Each type of crystal smells differently and most people can sense the subtle fragrance.
- Although they have all the common healing attributes of quartz crystals, they are focused strongly on self-healing (see page 61).

Blue mist Lemurian quartz crystals from Colombia are both grounding and uplifting.

- These crystals are instantly calming, both emotionally and physically, bringing a feeling of peacefulness. Some people report feeling tingling sensations through their hands, arms, and sometimes right through their whole body as soon as they hold a blue mist crystal.
- They promote confidence and help you to fulfill your ambitions, free from all the things that have ever held you back.
- They taste of clean water, like a natural mineral spring. It is a fresh and cleansing taste, which can give you a feeling of water running over stones. Try touching different areas of the crystal to the tip of your tongue and you'll discover that they taste different from one another. Always wash and cleanse your crystal first (see pages 128–132).
- Physically, they can assist in healing the lungs and heart, and are good for pain relief, especially when the pain is aggravated by stress, worry, and self-doubt. They can also aid fertility, balance hormones, and improve sex drive.

Blue mist Lemurian quartz is connected to the solar plexus chakra (see page 118).

Some blue mist crystals are "manifestation crystals," which is a term used to describe any crystal (typically quartz) that has another crystal growing inside it (which is often also, but not essentially, quartz) and is completely contained within the crystal, without touching the sides. Manifestation crystals are often very powerful tools for major life changes.

Manifestation crystals are specialists in bringing your dreams, goals, and desires into reality.

Self-healed Quartz Crystals

Blue mist Lemurian quartz crystals are self-healed crystals, which makes them perfect for self-healing and deep, inner healing work with clients. Crystals self-heal in two ways. The first, although still unusual, is more common. It occurs when a crystal termination has become damaged (which happens when a crystal breaks off from the cluster of its crystal family) and then starts to grow baby crystals from the damaged surface.

The second way is much rarer and is exemplified by blue mist Lemurian quartz crystals. Usually the "mist" inside a quartz crystal is created as the crystal forms and is due to natural imperfections in the structure as it grows. However, in blue mist crystals, this is not the case.

These crystals formed almost perfectly in the mountains of Colombia about 110 million years ago. Naturally, they are mostly optically clear. However, about 60 million years ago, there was a period of enormous geological activity on Earth, which internally fractured these crystals. After each of the Earth's tumultuous upheavals, the crystals healed themselves internally, giving rise to the appearance of the mist. The mist is accentuated when energy workers and crystal healers work with these crystals—the mist turns a pale blue color as the energy passes through the crystal.

The misty center of the blue mist Lemurian crystal is the self-healed area.

PRACTICAL EXERCISE:
MEDITATION JOURNEY INTO THE BLUE MIST

Meditating with a blue mist Lemurian crystal is grounding and uplifting at the same time, so it's an excellent crystal for anyone working on a creative project, a new relationship or business venture, or anything else you want to manifest into reality.

1. Make yourself comfortable in a quiet place where you won't be disturbed. Play some gentle meditative music to cover any distracting sounds and light a candle, if you wish.
2. Hold your blue mist Lemurian crystal and look at it. Examine the plays of light, its texture, the horizontal striations ("barcode" ridges) on the sides, the pointy termination at the top, and the rough bottom end. You can also hold the crystal to your ear and listen to its vibrations, smell it, and taste it on your tongue, but make sure you wash it first.
3. Once you feel that you really know your crystal, hold it upright and close your eyes. Take several slow, deep breaths and in your mind, imagine you are getting smaller and smaller with each breath, until there is a tiny you looking up at the giant crystal. Breathe for a moment and take in the immenseness of the blue mist Lemurian quartz crystal in front of which the tiny you is standing.
4. Start to walk around the base of the crystal and look for a way in. This might be a grandiose doorway or a simple, small wooden door. Maybe it's a window or just a gap in the crystalline wall. However you do it, enter the crystal.
5. Once inside, be aware of the murkiness and muddiness that the limonite creates in the crystal base. Move through this and let it pull away anything you don't need to hold on to—anything from your past, whether that's yesterday or a past life.
6. In your mind, start to ascend the crystal, moving through the mist. This might be via a glass elevator or an escalator, or you may find a staircase in the corner of the crystal, perhaps a massive, glamorous one or a tiny, rickety metal staircase. Whichever way, move up out of the murky limonite area and into the mystical, magical mist.
7. The mist starts to turn a pale blue as you continue your upward journey. As you move up through the crystal, its energy will move down through you. The blue mist envelops you, holding you like a gentle cloud of cotton wool, bathing the wounds from your past and reenergizing your soul.

8 The mist starts to clear, slowly at first, then more quickly as you approach the termination at the top of the crystal. Reaching the top, you can see out clearly over the landscape around you. Feel the freshness of the air, the brilliance of the Sun, and the clarity of your thoughts. As you stand in the apex of the crystal point, look around and see your answer…

9 You will then notice an inexplicable, but not uncomfortable, feeling as if you are growing. You will feel yourself getting bigger and bigger until you are sitting and holding your blue mist Lemurian crystal in your hands.

10 Gently open your eyes and become aware of your surroundings.

11 Cleanse the crystal (see pages 128–132) when you have finished.

Pink Variety (Colombia)

Pink Lemurian quartz crystals from Colombia have a special brightness that makes them "pop!" As well as hematite, they also have titanium inclusions, which give them their wow factor. On a metaphysical level, they help to connect your heart to the Earth, grounding the feeling of love, and at the same time they connect your heart to the heavens, opening your heart to new ways of seeing love. While this is happening, your heart chakra opens like the petals of a flower, allowing you to share this love with everyone around you and beyond. It is an amazing, freeing feeling for your body, mind, and spirit.

Pink Lemurian quartz from Colombia is connected to the heart chakra (see page 118).

Pink Colombian Lemurian quartz crystals will open your heart to love.

PRACTICAL EXERCISE:
LOVE MEDITATION

To start sharing the love within you, all you need is a quiet place, a pink Colombian Lemurian quartz crystal, and a little time.

1 Hold your crystal and take a few slow, deep breaths to center and ground yourself. Breathe in through your nose and out through your mouth.

2 Feel a loving energy build in your heart. Notice it connect to the Earth below you. Feel the nurture that the planet gives you.

3 Now let this loving energy connect to the sky above you. Feel your heart rising upward.

4 Let yourself simply enjoy this connection to the Earth and the sky for a moment.

5 When you feel ready, start to imagine a flower in your heart slowly opening its petals one by one. Soon there's a beautiful flower radiating love. Think about anyone you know who you would like to share some of this love with—picture the love flowing from the flower in your heart to the flower in theirs. You can repeat this step as often as you like for any number of people.

6 When you are finished, take three big, deep breaths and, each time you breathe out, blow away any emotions you may have picked up from the people you've sent your love to. This is because whenever you connect energetically with someone, there is always an energy exchange.

7 Cleanse the crystal (see pages 128–132) when you have finished.

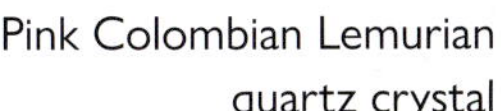

Pink Colombian Lemurian quartz crystal

Russian Lemurian Quartz Crystal

Discovered in September 2001 in the Ural Mountains in Russia, these were the first Lemurian crystals I encountered (see box below). Each time you work with Russian Lemurian quartz crystals, you feel extra-connected to the past because

The First Time I Met Lemurian Quartz Crystals

It was at the Tucson Gem Show in Arizona, USA, in February 2002 when I "discovered" these magical, mesmerizing Stone People. As I was walking through the outdoor section of the show in the beautiful, bright morning sunshine, suddenly and completely unexpectedly, a huge crystal display shone brighter and louder than I had ever experienced. Individually, the crystals shone out like beacons of light and all together they were enthralling.

I looked closer and noticed that as I approached them, some would sparkle as if they were waving and trying to attract my attention, while others would become dull as if they'd turned their light off to hide from me. I started selecting some of the crystals that sparkled at me. As I held each one, I felt a strong crystalline energy beyond anything I had felt before, but I also sensed something else that I couldn't quite put into words. Then, it dawned on me… I could hear names! The crystals were telling me their names! Except all the names were ones I recognized, and I soon realized they were all names of my customers, clients, and students. I was 5,000 miles (8,000 km) away from home and these crystals were telling me who they wanted to be with—wow! One of the crystals didn't tell me a name, but said it wanted to fly. I was returning to the UK a few days later and so, naturally, I thought it wanted to come with me.

these amazing crystals have layers of deep knowledge programmed within them. Your senses will be turned on and tuned in to an ancient age. Many people have profound life-changing experiences with these crystals.

As you can imagine, I'd been rather fond of these crystals and had overspent… and bought a lot of them! So, flying crystal had to stay, but another six crystals also hadn't told me a name, and I knew (without comprehending why) that they had to come with me. The day before I left, I returned to the seller to say farewell and he told me the crystal that wanted to fly had been bought by a pilot who was going to keep it in his cabin bag as he flew all over the world.

Back at my store in the UK, I unpacked all the Lemurian crystals, but rather than putting them on display, I placed them on tables in a private area upstairs. I then phoned the list of people whose names the crystals had spoken to me, and suggested they come to the store because I might have a special crystal for them. Over the next couple of weeks, each person came in and was shown upstairs. Every single one of them came down with the crystal that had said their name! Over the following months, occasionally a new customer would come into the store who I felt was destined for one of the six other crystals, so I'd ask if they wanted to look at some special crystals upstairs. Each person came down with one crystal, until all the crystals had found their new homes.

Smoky Lemurian Quartz Crystal

Occasionally, Lemurian quartz crystals from Russia (and Brazil—see below) can be smoky quartz, the brown coloration caused by natural radiation within the Earth. These crystals can be just as powerful as the non-smoky varieties and, as with all Lemurian crystals, they can be exceptionally bright.

One of their special features is that they are very protective when you are doing spiritual and shamanic work, be that healing yourself or others, or connecting to spirit or the divine. They reflect negativity which can be drawn to any focus of energy such as ceremony or healing work.

Smoky Lemurian quartz crystals are related to all the chakras, but particularly the base chakra. They are great for dreamwork (remembering and interpreting your nighttime dreams) and they help to turn dreams into reality.

Smoky Lemurian quartz is particularly associated with the base chakra (see page 118).

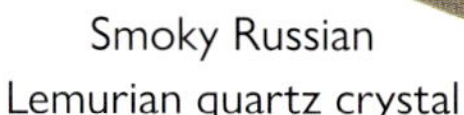

Smoky Russian Lemurian quartz crystal

Brazilian Lemurian Quartz Crystal

These were the first crystals identified as having a link to Lemuria in modern times. Discovered in the 1990s by crystal dealer David Geiger, it was Katrina Raphaell (a pioneer of contemporary crystal healing) who first called them Lemurian crystals. They come from the Serra do Cabral mountains in Minas Gerais, southeastern Brazil. They are usually clear quartz, but may also be golden (see page 69), red or pinkish (see pages 70–71), or occasionally smoky brown (see box above). The term "Lemurian seed crystal" was first attributed to Brazilian Lemurian quartz crystals that exhibited alternate frosted and brilliantly clear sides, with horizontal striations on the frosted sides but not on the clear sides. Not all Brazilian Lemurian crystals show this; many have horizontal striations on all sides.

Golden Variety (Brazil)

Although it may often look like citrine, which gets its color from heat within the ground, golden Lemurian quartz crystal from Brazil is, in fact, colored by iron inclusions. It is a particularly useful crystal when working on yourself, such as for self-healing or development. However, I have also found these crystals helpful when working with clients who need to release painful feelings or trauma from the past (see practical exercise below).

Golden Lemurian quartz from Brazil is linked to the solar plexus chakra (see page 118).

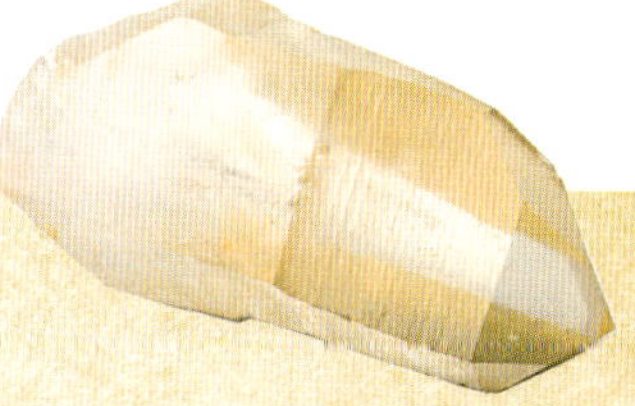

Golden Brazilian Lemurian quartz crystal

PRACTICAL EXERCISE:
RELEASE PAIN AND TRAUMA FROM THE PAST

This exercise will help to release the energy that's become stuck due to trauma or pain. It works just as well for both physical and emotional pain.

1. Sit comfortably and quietly in a space where you won't be disturbed.
2. Hold your golden Lemurian quartz crystal an inch or two away from your heart and move it slowly in a counterclockwise direction.
3. Continue for as long as you wish—you are likely to require several repetitions to complete the healing process.
4. Cleanse the crystal (see pages 128–132) when you have finished.

Remember, all healing is like an onion. You peel off one layer and there's another, then another. Be patient as you process each layer, one by one.

Red or Pink Variety (Brazil)

Colored by hematite or iron inclusions, red or pink Lemurian quartz crystals from Brazil are more grounding than any other Lemurian crystal variety (see practical exercise below). They're great to hold if you feel "spacey" when you are around lots of crystals or if you are doing any spiritual or psychic work. They can promote confidence and dependability, and can also help to relieve headaches and aid in the treatment of blood disorders.

PRACTICAL EXERCISE:
GROUND YOURSELF

Red or pink Lemurian quartz crystals from Brazil bring a grounding energy to any spiritual work, helping you to bring spiritual experiences into your everyday world. They help to keep your feet on the Earth as your spirit soars to explore. There are a couple of ways you can ground yourself with these crystals.

Pink Brazilian Lemurian quartz crystal

OPTION 1:

1 Hold the crystal in your right hand, with the termination pointing toward the ground.

2 Imagine any excess energy flowing from you through the crystal and into the ground. You can usually start to feel this working quickly.

3 Continue for 2–5 minutes.

4 Cleanse the crystal (see pages 128–132) when you have finished.

Red or pink Lemurian quartz from Brazil is associated with the base chakra (see page 118).

OPTION 2:

1 Place two red or pink Brazilian Lemurian crystals by your feet.
2 Close your eyes and take three slow, deep breaths.
3 Imagine you are standing next to a riverbank. In your mind, watch as you take off your shoes and socks.
4 See the red or pink crystals turn the riverbank you are standing on to mud and feel the mud squelch between your toes and around your feet.
5 After a few minutes, allow yourself to become aware of your surroundings again.
6 Cleanse the crystals (see pages 128–132) when you have finished.

Tibetan Quartz Crystal

These crystals commonly have black inclusions of carbon, manganese, or possibly hematite. Although there is some question as to whether or not they are Lemurian crystals, they do come from Tibet, and are therefore connected to the cataclysmic "bump" of the former island of India into Asia, which created the Himalayas and the Tibetan Plateau (see page 52). Tibet, situated on the Tibetan Plateau (the highest plateau on Earth), is commonly referred to as the "Roof of the World." Of all the crystals, Tibetan crystals are the ones closest to the gods. This is why they help with your spiritual connection to whatever you believe is helping and guiding you through this life. These crystals are also very good at directing you to slice through "waffle" and get to the point. Tibetan quartz crystals connect your heart and mind, and they are the perfect crystal to help you find the relationships you need, on any level and at any point in your life.

Working with Tibetan quartz in meditation will enhance your spiritual connection.

PRACTICAL EXERCISE:
THE CRYSTALLINE LEMURIAN ENERGY EXPERIENCE

For this exercise, you will need at least two (preferably more) Lemurian quartz crystals of any variety. You can enjoy this experience by yourself, but it's even better if there are at least two people. Some people receive deep healing (physical, emotional, mental, and spiritual) from this exercise and have amazing realizations about their health, life path, and themselves in general. Others are opened to self-discovery and inner reflection.

1 Lie on the floor, or on a bed, with all your Lemurian quartz crystals around you. As a minimum, you need two—one above your head pointing down and another below your feet pointing up, so that both crystals are pointing toward your body. Place any others in pairs on either side of your body, pointing in toward your chakras (see page 118).
2 Lie here for a few minutes. If you are doing this exercise with friends, then they can each take one of their own Lemurian quartz crystals, point it down toward your body, 2–12 in (5–30 cm) above any chakra point, and move it slowly in a clockwise direction for a few minutes.
3 Each person can continue until they feel that the person lying down has received enough crystalline Lemurian energy for now. Each crystal will let you know one way or another when it has had enough. You will feel a notable change in the crystal or within you. For example, the crystal might change temperature (hot to cold, or vice versa) or physically grind to a halt—it might start to feel as though you're pushing the crystal through treacle.
4 Give the person on the floor a little while to get up in their own time.
5 If you are in a group, then the next person can lie down and you can repeat the steps above. Keep doing so until each person has had a turn.
6 Cleanse the crystals (see pages 128–132) when you have finished.

Chapter 4

Ancient Knowledge and Inner Wisdom:

Accessing Past Lives and Answers from Within

Crystals are able to hold deep knowledge and so can act as powerful tools to help you unlock suppressed memories or feelings from the past that may be affecting you in the present. Certain crystals enable you to access deep wisdom from within, helping you to make sense of past lives and your current situation, and to provide insight for your future life path.

Past Lives

Many people have experiences and memories that they can't explain, often from a different period of history. Something is connecting them to a previous time. It can feel as though these experiences are real and even as if they are happening today. Some people think that these are past lives that the individual has lived before, while others suggest the idea of a collective group memory. Both of these thoughts would also explain the relatively common experience of meeting someone for the first time and feeling as if you have known them all your life.

Past lives have fascinated people from many cultures throughout history. The thought that we might have been here before explains why we have talents and abilities that seem innate. Some of these skills are passed on through our evolutionary development and are clearly genetic, but others cannot be explained so simply. Having had past lives also implies that you will have a future life and gives a basis for life-after-death, which poses the question "What next?" Beliefs vary; some suggest that we return to Earth in human form, others in human or animal form depending on the merit we have gained, or lost, by our actions in this life. This concept is known as karma in Sanskrit.

Another question that has been posed over time is: "Are we only affected by our deeds in each life we live or do our actions in previous lives carry forward to the next?" In other words, does karma exist? Will our acts in this incarnation affect us in the next?

The Buddhist Wheel of Life is a representation of *samsara*—the continuous circle of life, death, and rebirth.

Different traditions have similar ways of expressing these ideas. Buddhists have the Wheel of Life with its depiction of the realms of *samsara*, the continuous circle of life, death, and rebirth. Shamanic traditions often refer to "soul pools" —the idea that our soul is part of a pool of conscious energy—rather than any form of individual reincarnation. Whatever view is followed, there is an energy link between each life and the energy itself is transformed and transmuted by the events it experiences and carries.

Crystals for Accessing Past Lives

Certain crystals (see pages 79–82) can assist in past-life recall. Working with these crystals can help you to remember and review your past lives with clarity and understanding. Experiment with them until you find the one(s) that work for you. Try holding the crystal every day for just 10–20 minutes (or longer if preferred), or you could carry the crystal with you, meditate with it, or place it on your nightstand or under your pillow while you sleep.

Recalling memories from past lives can facilitate healing in your current life.

Petrified Wood

Perhaps the most notable crystal to aid past-life work, and past-life recall, is petrified wood, also known as fossil wood or fossilized wood. The word "petrified" literally means "turned to stone." Petrified wood forms when one or more mineral replaces the original material of the tree. Many shamanic rituals employ this crystal to facilitate and enhance past-life regression. This can be done in two ways, very generally by either shamanic regression (using traditional shamanic practices to create an altered state and journey into the past) or hypnotic regression (done under hypnosis). Whichever route you take, the experiences are remembered and can be used to facilitate healing and understanding of events and disease in this life.

Apatite

This is another crystal that promotes recall and understanding of past-life events.

Alexandrite

Sometimes, issues from our past lives can affect us in our present lives. Alexandrite can help you to leave such troubles behind and move forward. Working with alexandrite can occasionally lead to big emotional or spiritual changes and reactions, such as a rebirth.

Boulder Opal

Another helpful crystal is boulder opal, which can assist in bringing past-life recall from the subconscious to the conscious mind, and by putting current issues or situations into perspective, allowing you to view them with increased understanding. This gives you the power of rational thought and enables you to move forward and make more balanced decisions.

Dioptase

We may carry all sorts of feelings with us from the past, some of which can be detrimental, such as feelings of oppression or guilt. Working with dioptase will help to gently release these emotions.

Recalling past lives can be a deeply awakening and transformative experience.

Unakite

Sometimes, people feel as though they have lost something, but can't quite put their finger on what they've lost or when this happened. This might suggest that pain is lodged in a past life, which isn't related to their present life. This feeling is often related to the loss of a goal or idea, perhaps in relation to a relationship or career. It is often not the loss itself that is important but what the loss represented. For example, the loss of a job may be linked, on a deep-past life level, to freedom.

If you are experiencing such feelings of loss, unakite will open the locked doors in your heart and mind, which will lead to the answers you seek. You should note that it is not always the case that such a loss is linked to past-life experiences; being unable to place a loss may instead be related to a traumatic event in this life which has been suppressed.

Eudialyte

We may have committed an act in a past life that we deeply regret, and we might hold on to this feeling from one existence to the next. We can be linked to people through several lifetimes: friends or enemies that we keep meeting who help or hinder our progress. We can hold karmic grudges. Eudialyte can help you to let go of these connections and love anew or forgive as you need to.

Spirit Quartz

This crystal can help you to let go of past-life experiences that might be linked to current obsessive behaviors. This will give you a new sense of belonging, which can help you to enter new social groups and make friends.

Cerussite

Helping to ground past-life experiences in the present, cerussite enables you to see and understand how these affect you now. Using this knowledge, you will be able to free yourself from limiting ties, heal past hurts, and move forward in your present life with more confidence to live life to the full every day.

TIP

If you are in any doubt about past-life experiences affecting you in your present life, speak to a crystal therapist, or other therapist or counselor specializing in past-life healing or recall.

One of My Past-life Experiences

I have had several memories or feelings about past lives that I may have experienced, but the first time I physically experienced a past life was in the 1990s on my first trip to Scotland, UK. My then wife and I had driven to Scotland overnight. As we drove close to the battlefield of Culloden near Inverness in the early morning, for a moment, I felt as though I had physically died. I stopped the car and walked back to the exact spot in which I had experienced this feeling. In this location, it was April 16, 1746, and I was a priest healing wounded soldiers from the Battle of Culloden when I was murdered. I felt this as if it was actually happening to me in that moment. If I took two steps forward from this position, I returned to the twentieth century; back two steps and it was the eighteenth century!

Returning to the car, I told my wife that I knew a great place we could get breakfast. I had never been to Scotland, and this was before the days of the internet and smartphones, so I had no way of looking it up, but somehow I knew where to go. We drove off down a small road and then turned onto a track. After a little way, we came to an old manor house, which had been converted into a modern hotel and they had just started serving breakfast! I spoke to the owners about the hotel and they told me it had several secret passages and a priest hole. The manor house had belonged to a Jacobite family who had supported Charles Edward Stuart and the Jacobite uprising against English rule! Wow! I have since had other similar past-life experiences in different places around the world.

PRACTICAL EXERCISE:

A PAST-LIFE EXPERIENCE MEDITATION

To access one of your past lives, you will need a piece of petrified wood. If you don't have one, you can focus on the image on this page. You will also need a pen and a piece of paper or a mobile device to record your experience as soon as you finish. Please read through all the instructions before you begin.

I have written two very different pieces of music that will enhance this experience. These can be streamed from any music streaming service (see page 138 for details). *In the Footsteps of the Ancestors*, a piece of music from my album *Walking the Walk*, is six minutes long and is perfect to help you start to experience the possibility of a past life. For a deeper, hour-long experience, listen to my album *A Shaman's Drumming Journey* while practicing this exercise.

1 Place your piece of petrified wood close by, so it is within easy reach. Dim the lights and press play on your music player.

2 Sitting comfortably or lying down, close your eyes and take three deep breaths into your belly. You can place your hands on your tummy and feel your abdomen expand as you breathe in and let your hands fall away as you exhale.

3 Focus on the middle of your mind and watch any thoughts or worries float away. If they feel stuck, imagine that each thought is in a balloon and that you are holding the strings. Allow yourself to let go of each string and watch the balloons float away.

4 When your mind is clear, think back in time. Follow your life backward. Visualize any major life events and any memories you have; you might be surprised by what comes to mind. Just go with it. Keep going all the way back through adolescence, childhood, infancy, and being born. Follow this thought right back into the womb. Let yourself be in this calm, warm, safe place for a while.

Petrified wood

5. When you feel ready, imagine watching yourself being born into a different time in the past. Follow your thoughts as you experience being in this time period.
6. When the music ends, become aware of your body, from your toes through your feet and legs and into your fingers, hands, and arms, all the way up your body to the top of your head. Gently open your eyes and bring your focus back into the room.
7. Immediately write down or record whatever you recall from your experience. If you can't remember anything, start with how you are feeling and how different areas of your body feel. You will likely remember more as you start to write.

You can repeat this exercise many times to shed more light on individual experiences and to explore multiple past lives.

Remember to cleanse your piece of petrified wood after you have worked with it (see pages 128–132).

Crystal Guides

Everyone has energetic helpers with them. Some people like to call them spirit guides, angels, guardians, deities, ancestors, star beings, nature spirits, totem or spirit animals, or ascended masters.

I believe that everyone has several spirit guides who help them with different aspects through life. Some guides, like guardian angels, want to look after you and some want to help your spiritual development. Others, such as crystal guides, may be more interested in helping you with something specific. In my experience, as soon as someone starts to work with crystals, a new guide will be helping them. Some people will be aware of their guide straight away; others will discover their presence later.

When I am teaching crystal healing, I find that my students often say things such as "I feel like I remember this, but I don't know where from," "I know this but I don't know why," and "It all seems so familiar, as if I've done this before." Similarly, sometimes, I think I have a great new idea; a different technique for working with crystals, which works fabulously for the clients who need it. And then, a while later—sometimes hours, days, weeks, or months—I have a feeling that it's been done before. My crystal guide lets me know that it really wasn't my idea at all! Just as I remind my students of things they know from another time, I am reminded, too.

My crystal spirit guide, Man Who Sits With Stones, revealed himself to me over 30 years ago and, for a long time, he was quite an enigma. He definitely held a wealth of knowledge about crystals but would sometimes have slightly bizarre and ritualistic ways of doing things, which I felt should be quite simple. One of my most memorable experiences with him is detailed on page 88.

Man Who Sits With Stones

I once had—or thought I'd had—an amazing revelation about a new and powerful way of applying crystals for healing. My science brain kicked in (I have a bachelor's degree in Applied Biology) and thought that for a physical injury, if a crystal could be placed on or near to the area it is trying to treat, then surely it would be more effective than if it was being worn or carried. So, in meditation, I consulted Man Who Sits With Stones.

I explained my idea, that I could tape a flat crystal to the skin at or near the site of injury with micropore surgical tape and it would speed up healing. His response was almost shocking. "No, no, no, no, no!" he said. "You must take a soft fur, like rabbit, to wrap the stone. You can also add aloe vera, chamomile, or moss if the wound is open. Then you bind the dressing you have made to the area with soft leather strips from either goat or deer." I knew that the plants have antibacterial properties, but really didn't understand the whole binding ritual. "But why can't I use micropore tape?" I said.

"No, no, no, no, no!" he replied, getting slightly irritated at my lack of understanding. "You must take a soft fur, like rabbit, to wrap the stone. Then you bind the dressing you have made to the area with soft leather strips from either goat or deer," he reiterated, this time leaving out the plants to simplify things for his foolish student.

"But why can't I just use micropore..." "No!" he interrupted, now getting more irate and once again describing his method. This went on for a while... Some days later, I had a thought. I asked if he knew what micropore surgical tape was. He didn't! I went to the bathroom and produced some. I took a flattish crystal and taped it to my leg. Man Who Sits With Stones looked at me, and after a few moments said in a very matter-of-fact way, "Oh, okay. Why don't you use that then?"

I believe we have a deep memory from the past. Whether this is from past lives, soul pools, or genetic inheritance does not matter; it is only important that we remember. For years, Man Who Sits With Stones was an enigma. Other than being of Native American heritage and having a love of crystals and healing, I didn't know anything else about him. Then, around the turn of the century, I was at the Tucson Gem and Mineral Show in Arizona, USA, and I took a day off to visit the Tohono O'odham people on the San Xavier Reservation. There, I learned about an ancient civilization called the Hohokam, who lived in a large area extending from South-Central Arizona, USA, all the way down into Sonora, Mexico, between 300 and 1500 CE. The Hohokam were technically advanced compared to other peoples in the area at the time, building cities and irrigation canals that stretched for hundreds of miles.

San Xavier del Bac Mission, Tucson, Arizona, USA

I realized that Man Who Sits With Stones comes from the Hohokam civilization, not just in terms of the area and locally available crystals that he likes to work with, but also in that his technical knowledge is limited to his own time, which was demonstrated by his insistence that I must "Take a soft fur, like rabbit, to wrap the stone. Then you bind the dressing you have made to the area with soft leather straps from either goat or deer" (see box opposite). But today we have this magical invention of surgical tape which we take for granted.

PRACTICAL EXERCISE:

DISCOVER AND CONNECT WITH YOUR CRYSTAL GUIDE

For this exercise, you will need either an aqua aura or lapis lazuli crystal. Both will work well to help you connect with your crystal guide and receive a message from them.

1 Find a quiet time and space where you won't be disturbed. Sit quietly for a moment and allow yourself to breathe. Take a few slow, deep breaths down into your belly, so you can center your being and give your mind permission to clear. Stop thinking about everyday things and let any thoughts, stresses, and worries float away.

2 Focus on your crystal. Just look at it and, if you are holding it, be aware of how it feels in your hands.

3 Imagine your crystal filling with blue light. Picture this blue light flowing into you until it completely fills you and you are glowing with a blue aura around you. Blue is the color of communication and also the color associated with guides you haven't yet found.

4 Focus on the blueness inside and around you, connecting with your crystal guide who is sharing their energy in your aura.

5 In your quiet, blue inner space, listen with all your senses; be aware of anything you may see, hear, feel, smell, and taste, and receive the message from your crystal guide. It might be heard or seen or sensed or felt, or just known with an inner knowing… it doesn't matter how.

6 Record your experience and any message from your crystal guide for future reference.

Aqua aura

You can repeat this exercise whenever you want a helping hand on your crystal journey.

Remember to cleanse your crystal after you have worked with it (see pages 128–132).

Lapis lazuli

Akasha and the Akashic Records

The idea of Akasha comes from Hindu tradition. Akasha is a Sanskrit word, which can mean "ether," "space," or "spirit." It is thought of as a hidden fifth element, and the origin of the other four elements: Earth, Air, Fire, and Water. Akasha is everywhere and is the foundation and essence of everything that exists. It is a vast, limitless force of energy that permeates everything, yet cannot be seen or touched.

From this comes the concept of the Akashic Records, which can be thought of as a massive storage system. Perhaps it is the biggest etheric supercomputer memory bank or the most gigantic library you can imagine, which holds all the knowledge and information from the past, present, and future—in fact, it contains all there is to know. Not just events, but every thought, feeling, and idea ever experienced.

Some say that only "very special people" can see these buildings, computers, or energy fields, but really, anyone can access the Akashic Records through a simple spiritual practice and a seemingly magical key (see pages 94–95).

You can only ever access a tiny proportion of the knowledge available. This is limited to what you need to know for your soul at the time and is not necessarily what you would like to know for your physical form. Often, people look to the Akashic Records for an "answer" to a "question," but in the energetic reality in which the Records exist, you don't actually know the question that needs answering, and so the answer is often not what you expect!

PRACTICAL EXERCISE:

RUBY MEDITATION TO UNLOCK THE AKASHIC RECORDS

To connect to the Akashic Records, you will need a magical key—a record keeper ruby crystal with natural, raised triangles on its termination. (If you don't have one of these rubies, you can imagine one as in the photo opposite.) You will also need a pen and a piece of paper or a mobile device to record your experience.

1 Find a quiet, comfortable place where you won't be disturbed and hold (or imagine you are holding) your record keeper ruby crystal.

2 Take three deep breaths. With each exhalation, let go of anything that is stressing or worrying you. Now breathe normally and allow yourself to relax for a moment.

3 Imagine you are walking into bright white light. Everything around you is bright white light. You can sense an invisible wall in front of you. Approach it slowly until you can feel it with your hands. Follow the wall until you reach an invisible door. You will feel the edge of the door and a hexagonal lock. Insert your hexagonal ruby crystal into the lock and turn it counterclockwise. The door becomes visible and opens.

4 You step into a bright white room, which you realize is an elevator. There are no controls, only lights at the top designating floors. The elevator goes up and you watch as the floor numbers go higher and higher, through tens, hundreds, and eventually into the thousands.

5 The elevator stops. The door opens and you step out. You are in a library. Perhaps it is a classic, old-fashioned library filled with ancient tomes or something more modern in design, made of glass, and filled with computer terminals. You are approached by the librarian, who, without you saying

anything, guides you to the relevant section. There is a reading chair, desk, lamp, and a cup filled with your favorite drink. The librarian places a book, e-reader, or perhaps some bright white light on the desk. You start to read.

6 After some time, the librarian reappears, telling you it is time to go. The book, chair, desk, lamp, and cup all disappear. You find yourself in the bright white elevator. It is descending, the floor numbers above you dropping rapidly. The elevator stops on the ground floor and, as you step out, you can sense the invisible door in the invisible wall. Everything else is bright white light. You put your ruby crystal in the lock and turn it clockwise. The door opens. You step through the door and back into your mind.

7 As you breathe, start to become aware of the ruby crystal that you are holding or imagining. Become aware of your fingers, hands, and arms, and slowly allow yourself to recognize how you are feeling.

8 When you feel ready, open your eyes and bring your focus slowly back. Make a note of your experience and any information you have received.

Remember to cleanse your ruby crystal after you have worked with it (see pages 128–132).

Hexagonal ruby crystal

Divination

It is a human instinct to think about the future and to want to know what's going to happen next, be that in an hour, tomorrow, next week, or next year. We all want to know. I believe this stems from prehistoric times when predicting future events, such as the weather and routes taken by migrating herds, was essential to survival. It is thought that crystals and stones may well have been part of the earliest human divination tools, as well as animal bones and other artifacts.

People have been seeking the answer to "life, the Universe, and everything" (as the author Douglas Adams puts it) since the dawn of humankind. The shaman or seer who could predict the future was held in high esteem within the community. This goes back in time much further than *Homo sapiens* and was probably a very early development of our ancient hominin ancestors.

Whether divining the future by casting crystals, observing the signs of nature, or reading the entrails of sheep, prophecy and prediction are human second nature. We have all had experiences when we have "known" something is about to happen and it amazingly does. Sometimes these can be quite mundane things like thinking someone is about to call you, and suddenly the phone rings and it is them. And sometimes these premonitions are about much deeper, life-enhancing or life-changing events. Is this experience, or an inner knowing coming from the depths of our soul, or a connection to a divine being?

Crystals have been, and still are, employed by people all around the world as a way of contacting their gods, ancestors, and spirits to discover answers. The Ndembu people living in Zambia have been known to use divination baskets—a practice that has been passed down from their ancestors. This literally involves a basket filled with crystals, other natural objects such

One method of divination involves observing and interpreting signs from nature.

as bones and sticks, and anything else that catches the doctor's (*chimbuki*) eye on their travels. They've been known to include pull tabs from soda cans and pieces of brightly colored plastic, each item in the basket having a specific spiritual meaning. The items are either picked out seemingly at random to answer a specific query or cast from the basket onto the floor for a deeper answer.

Dowsing

An ancient form of divination, dowsing comes from the idea of water divining, which is a practice used to locate water, traditionally with a dowsing rod made from a forked (Y-shaped) twig or a crystal or stone on the end of a piece of string or leather. Modern dowsing tools include crystal pendulums or metal dowsing rods. All of these tools follow the same principle of answering a question with either "yes" or "no."

In ancient times, forked twigs were used to find water. Shamans would have asked, "Is there water here?" and then walked in the direction the spirits guided them until they received a "yes" answer from their stick. Water companies around the world are still dowsing for water to this day, using modern dowsing rods to find underground pipes or to locate leaks.

We are all descended from people who could dowse (they found water and survived, while others who couldn't dowse didn't survive), so we all have the ability to dowse. Some people are naturally better at it than others, just as some people are better at playing the piano or writing poetry than others, but with practice you will improve. The crystal pendulum is my favorite dowsing tool. Crystals enhance everything you do, so naturally will nurture and improve your innate dowsing ability.

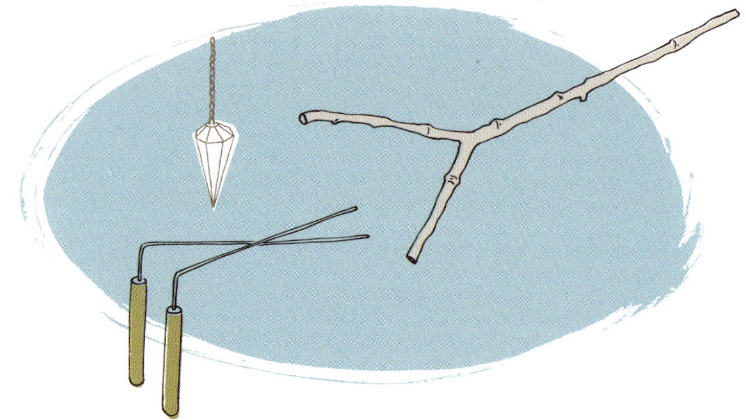

A forked twig, dowsing rods, and a crystal pendulum are all effective dowsing tools.

PRACTICAL EXERCISE:
CHOOSING A PENDULUM

While it's possible to select a pendulum online, it is best to do so in a physical store that has a good selection to choose from.

1 Still your body and mind and let any emotions that are affecting you float away.

2 When you feel calm and relaxed, look at the selection of pendulums in front of you and select the first one you notice, or the one that jumps out at you. Don't be afraid of your intuition—you will know the answer if you let yourself.

3 Once you have picked the pendulum, you need to identify your "yes" and "no" responses. Hold the chain and ask the pendulum to show you a "yes." The pendulum will move one of four ways: clockwise, counterclockwise, forward and backward, or side to side. Whichever way the pendulum moves, this is your "yes" response.

4 Then ask the pendulum to show you a "no" response, and you will see one of the other three possible movements.

5 If you prefer, you can ask a question that has a definitive answer, such as "Is my name [say your name]?" This will identify the "yes" response. Then ask the same question using a different name to identify the "no" response.

6 Once you have identified the "yes" and "no" responses, the first question to ask your new pendulum friend is: "Are you a good pendulum for me to work with?" Hopefully it says "yes." If so, you have chosen your pendulum. If it answers "no," select a different pendulum and start the process again until you find your pendulum.

Now that you've chosen your pendulum, you can start to ask it questions. See page 100 for some tips on how to do this.

Tips for Working With Your Pendulum

You can ask your pendulum anything you like, but here are a few points to bear in mind.

- If you find it difficult to get your pendulum to start moving, try grounding yourself by holding hematite in your other hand as you ask your questions.
- Your pendulum will always answer in the moment and never predict the future. For example, if you and a friend are on your way to meet for lunch, your pendulum will accurately tell you if the lunch will happen or not. But if you ask your pendulum whether you and 20 friends will get together in a year's time for a reunion dinner, the answer you receive will not necessarily tell you what will happen in a year. The answer you get is in this moment, which, in this example, is: right now, do you and your 20 friends intend to get together for a reunion dinner next year? And not what will happen next year.

Hematite will help to ground you.

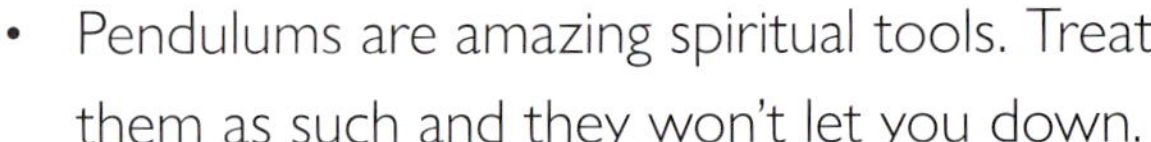

- Pendulums are amazing spiritual tools. Treat them as such and they won't let you down.
- Don't ask your pendulum the same question over and over again. It will get bored and start giving you different answers.
- Pendulums don't like frivolous questions and they also don't support greed, anger, or hatred. If your question is important to you, it is not frivolous, even if others might think so. If you are asking a question to help you or others, that's good too.

A crystal pendulum will help you to tune in to your intuition.

How NOT to Treat a Pendulum!

Many years ago, when I started working in the crystal world, I did my very first newspaper interview with a skeptical reporter. By the end of the interview, she was so convinced and amazed by the pendulum I had shown her that she bought one herself and took it back to her office.

The next day, she phoned me, sounding very distressed. She said that when she showed her coworkers the pendulum, some of them had laughed at her. She wanted to prove to them that it worked, so decided to bet on a horse race. The reporter and her coworkers each contributed £1 (about $1.30) and bet on a winner. They used the pendulum to predict the winning horse… and it won! So they decided to bet on another race, each contributing £100 (about $130) and… the horse lost! Now the reporter's on the phone to me, telling me her colleagues are very angry with her and asking me what she should do! I suggested that they should bet on another horse race, each contributing £100 again, but this time, before predicting the winner with the pendulum, they should agree on a charity that they will give all the winnings to. They did, and this time, the horse won.

The point of this tale is that it explains how pendulums work. For the first bet, the pendulum was just proving that it worked. Since the second bet was placed for pure greed, the pendulum, just like any spiritual tool, was not interested in helping. The final time, the colleagues reverted to a good intention and won. So why can't we all just win money for charities every day? Well, that puts a judgment on good and bad—which charity does good; which is corrupt or has political associations and implications; whether you are donating the money for personal gain; and many other biases.

Pendulums only answer yes or no. They have no consideration of good or bad, if such things really exist anyway.

PRACTICAL EXERCISE:
CONNECT TO YOUR INNER PENDULUM

We all have an inner pendulum. It's located in your gut: your sacral chakra (see page 118). We usually only sense it in extreme moments, but it is working round the clock. If you listen to your inner pendulum, it will guide you. You can connect to it anywhere, anytime, and in any position (standing, seated, or lying down), but it's easier if you are seated or standing in a quiet place where you won't be disturbed.

1 Close your eyes and take a few slow, deep breaths to still, center, and focus yourself.
2 Imagine the happiest thing that's ever happened to you. Picture it—the person or people there, what you were doing, the sights, sounds, smells, tastes, and feelings.
3 Notice an energy rising from your sacral chakra up toward your heart, or maybe it goes even higher to the top of your head. Hold this feeling for a moment. Then let it go. This is your "yes" from your inner pendulum.
4 Take a few more slow, deep breaths to bring you back to a neutral point. You might find it helpful to place your hands on your sacral chakra.

5 Now imagine an uncomfortable or sad situation, or one that made you feel afraid. Picture it—the person or people there, what you were doing, the sights, sounds, smells, tastes, and feelings. Notice an energy sinking from your sacral chakra toward your base or even lower, right down to your feet. Hold this feeling for a moment. Then let it go. This is your "no" from your inner pendulum.

You will feel your inner pendulum in your sacral chakra (see page 118).

6 Repeat these steps a few times until you recognize the feelings as soon as they start to occur. Try imagining different scenarios in each category, too.

7 Try practicing this exercise in the real world. In your normal day, be aware of the up "yes" and the sinking "no" feelings inside you. Add your crystal pendulum, too, because every time you see it moving in front of you, it will reinforce your recognition of the feeling inside you.

This exercise will help you to make the right decisions for you all day long, from the mundane to the life-changing ones. The more you practice, the easier it gets—your confidence will increase and you will learn to trust yourself.

Chapter 5

Crystal Healing:

From Ancient Origins to the Modern Age

Crystals have been worked with by medicine people and shamans around the world for thousands of years, the results of which are reported throughout history. The healing abilities of crystals are attested to by an ever-growing bank of anecdotal evidence. Today, people from all parts of the globe have a natural affinity for and knowledge of crystals and their universal healing powers.

The History and Traditions of Crystal Healing

Some of the oldest spiritual applications of crystals have been found in burial sites of the earliest people—the discovery of carnelian beads in ancient graves (see page 11) indicates a belief that crystals were important for the soul's journey to the next life. Over 100,000 years ago, humans were collecting crystals and transporting them many miles to sacred sites to enhance the special natural energy found there (see page 14). Ancient civilizations, from Lemuria and Atlantis to Egypt and Greece, have all applied crystals to their spiritual beliefs and as healing tools.

Mesopotamia

In Mesopotamia, which encompasses present-day Iraq and parts of Iran, Syria, and Turkey, crystals were worked with for divination (see page 97). This was probably achieved by casting (throwing) crystals on the ground or onto a table and interpreting the patterns and meanings assigned to the types of crystals.

Additionally, the Mesopotamians crafted rose quartz into jewelry and decorative homewares, as well as into powerful amulets designed to attract love and to heal emotional scars and wounds. This may be one of the earliest records of a specific healing application of crystals.

Rose quartz is still a popular crystal for making jewelry today.

The Chaldeans of the Mesopotamian region were the first people to kindle the concept of birthstones, linking specific crystals to planets and, in turn, their association with times of the year (see pages 44–49). The idea is that when you are born, the celestial bodies such as the Sun, the Moon, planets, and stars create a specific energetic vibration in the Universe so wearing or carrying your birthstone recreates the vibrations of the Universe at the time you were born, which will bring you good health and happiness. Interestingly, there is some circumstantial evidence that many people find good things happen to them around the time of their birthday.

Ancient Egypt

The ancient Egyptians mined for crystals and gems and used them to make jewelry and amulets, which were often used as protective talismans. They believed that applying crystals to the body enhanced their potential, so crystals were worn to ensure the well-being of the wearer. The scarab beetle was a popular amulet because it was a symbol of life and rebirth, and so the deceased would often be buried with these amulets, with the belief that it would protect them in the afterlife.

Crystals were also used for their metaphysical properties. For example, lapis lazuli and malachite were ground up and made into pastes to use as eye shadow to enhance the wearer's clairvoyance (clear seeing). There were almost certainly earlier methods like this in use by shamanic cultures around the world before records began.

Ancient Egyptian jewelry was decorated with an abundance of crystals—in this case, possibly lapis lazuli, turquoise, citrine, mother of pearl, amethyst, amber, jasper, gold, quartz, and chalcedony.

Mesoamerica and South America

Obsidian knife

Ancient civilizations of Mexico and Central and South America, including the Olmec, Toltec, Maya, Aztec, and Inca, employed crystals such as obsidian and turquoise extensively in their spiritual rituals. In these cultures, offering the heart from a sacrifice (often human) was thought to bring favor from the gods. Obsidian knives were the tool of choice. Their shamans also employed obsidian knives for surgery in their healing practices because exceptionally sharp blades can be made from obsidian. Interestingly, in the 1980s, surgical blades made from obsidian started to be used in some plastic surgery procedures and are still used for the most delicate procedures because obsidian can be sharpened significantly more finely than the steel blades of conventional scalpels.

Samaria

From Samaria, an ancient region of Israel, we have the knowledge of crystal elixirs. The word "elixir" is derived from Arabic and means "magical liquid." A crystal elixir is made by placing a crystal in water (or other drinkable liquid), leaving it for a period of time, and then removing the crystal. The essence of the crystal's energy is left in the elixir—when it is drunk, the crystal's power will work from within the body. Crystal elixirs can be very effective in treating some conditions, such as an amber elixir for constipation or a rose quartz elixir for signs of aging in the skin.

China

Traditional Chinese Medicine employs many crystals. Examples include jade to revitalize the body's vital energy, help detoxification, and reduce inflammation; amethyst to relieve stomach pains and dispel bad dreams; citrine to ease emotional upsets and digestive disorders; tourmaline, which is linked to the balance of yin and yang energies and ceremonies; and lapis lazuli for congestion, spasms, and lymphatic ailments.

Europe

Preseli bluestone (spotted dolerite rock with feldspar and other minerals forming the spots) was used in the original construction of Stonehenge, which is a prehistoric stone circle in England, in the UK. Gray-green in color when dry, it naturally and magically turns blue when wet. A truly magical stone! It is thought that chippings from the Preseli bluestones were given by priests to people seeking healing for all sorts of conditions.

During the Middle Ages, various precious stones were believed to have medicinal properties and so were worked with in healing practices. These were documented in popular texts called lapidaries. John Dee, a sixteenth-century English mathematician and astrologer, had a crystal which he claimed was given to him by the angel Uriel and was later used to heal illnesses.

Stonehenge was, and still is, an important spiritual site for Britons.
Preseli bluestone (right) was used in its original construction.

How Does Crystal Healing Work?

Crystal healing is easy—it's not rocket science. Well, actually, as we saw in Chapter 1, it is! We only have rockets in space because of the crystals employed in technology, such as quartz in clocks, rubies in lasers, and crystalline silicon in solar cells. Despite all these scientific discoveries, the way in which crystals work for healing purposes is still a bit of a mystery. But that is not to say they don't work.

Although there is little "scientific" evidence that crystal healing works, there is plenty of anecdotal evidence, with people reporting improvements in their emotional, physical, and mental health. In my experience, everyone who follows a complete course of crystal healing notices an improvement in their well-being.

A Comparison in Science

Trying to prove that crystal healing works is a little bit like a nuclear physicist trying to prove the existence of a subatomic particle. The subatomic particle cannot be seen with any optical equipment that exists. However, by creating and repeating many experiments, it is possible to track other larger particles and record these. By following the tracks of these larger particles, the physicist can see that another particle has collided with or exerted a force on the subatomic particles. The physicist can then calculate the forces involved in these collisions and describe the invisible subatomic particle by its effect. This is anecdotal evidence of the particle's existence since the same effect may be caused by other unknown energies.

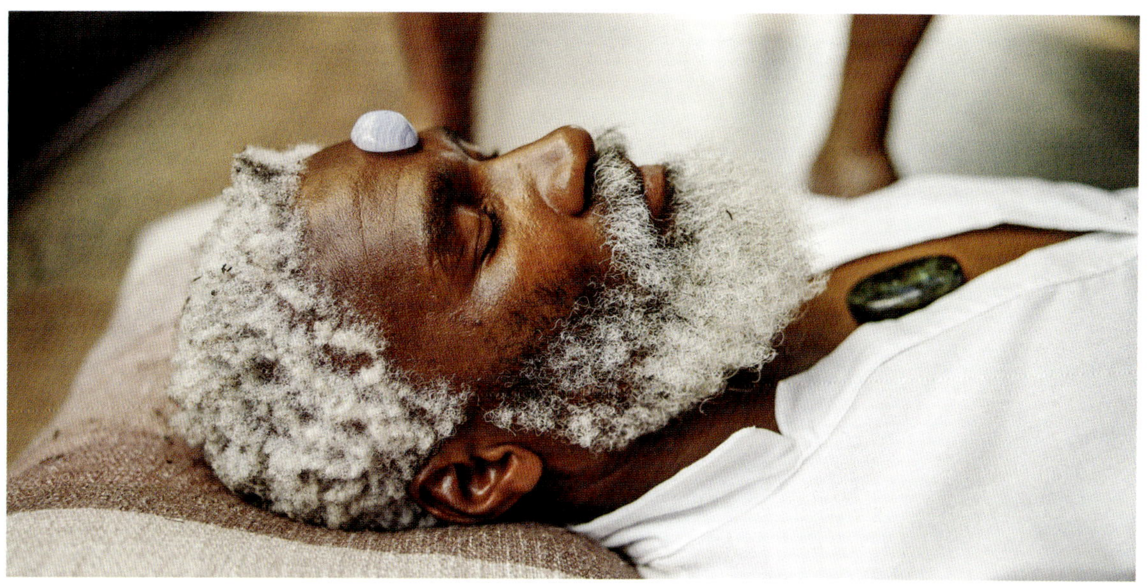

Placing crystals on the body is one method of crystal healing.

The theory of crystal healing is that crystals work by bringing balance to the body's energy system (see pages 115–120), which is composed of the aura, the energy field that surrounds the body; the chakras, the body's energy hot spots; and the meridians, channels for energy to flow through the body.

With crystal healing, the client's state of well-being improves. Symptoms—often chronic (long-term)—stop. Changes manifest in their lives, promoting health and recovery. By observing the client, it is evident that some form of force or energy has been involved, and it is the observed effects that are proof of its efficacy. Yet most people (with the exception of shamans and energy workers) cannot actually see the energy being directed through the crystal. It is possible that forces are being generated on a subatomic level, which create these positive changes in the client.

Skeptical Viewpoint

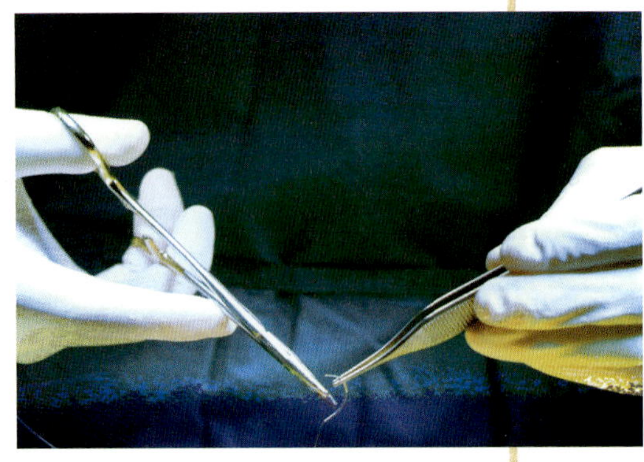

People who doubt the efficacy of crystal healing might argue that there is no scientific study to prove it, by which they usually mean a double-blind test. And you could reply that millions of people—estimated at 310 million people around the world—have surgery each year and yet there has never been a scientific study like a double-blind test for its effectiveness! You see, to do this, surgeons would have to take two groups of people with a specific illness or medical condition, and operate on all of them, giving half of them the correct surgical procedure, such as repair or removal of damaged tissue, while the other half undergo the same surgical motions during the same length of time inside their body, but without the corrective surgery, before being sewn back up. Of course, you would also need a control group with the same number of people who were healthy and give them the same operation as the first group, cutting into healthy flesh and removing the undamaged tissue or organ!

Research has shown that distant healing with crystals does have an effect on patients, and there is evidence that the operator and observer of an experiment have an influence on the outcome. So, with the help of a trained crystal therapist and a loving relative or friend, combined with the ability of crystals to work in distant healing, crystal therapy is an effective, noninvasive, holistic healing modality. Some scientists have stopped dismissing the idea that a rock can heal, and are willing to look again at the beneficial effects of crystals, which have been known by shamans and medicine people around the world for thousands of years.

Universal Life Force Energy

Where does the energy come from that the body needs to physically function? According to medicine, the *only* significant source of energy for all the physical processes and activities within the body is a biochemical reaction that takes place in the body's cells. Adenosine triphosphate (ATP) breaks down to adenosine diphosphate (ADP) and releases energy, then an enzyme (a type of protein that speeds up chemical reactions) helps it loop back to ATP.

However, as every first year medical or biology student will tell you, this only produces about 20 percent of the energy the adult human needs to exist. *There is no other significant scientifically proven source of energy for the body.* So where does the other 80 percent come from?

If I told you there was a power, an energy in the Universe, that makes up the majority of everything in the cosmos, including you and I, the seat you are sitting on, the pages of this book you're reading right now, the light in the room, the air that you breathe, and everything else, would you believe me? Oh, and you couldn't see it, but it affects everything you do, see, think, and feel.

It has been known in many cultures, through all ages, that there is an omnipresent force in the Universe. In China, it is called *chi*, in India *prana*, and in Japan *ki*. Some Native American cultures may call it Great Spirit, and many faiths, such as Christianity and Hinduism, believe that a God exists everywhere and within all things. In quantum physics, it might be called dark energy (see page 114). I will call it *chi*, but whatever you choose to call it, it is essential to life. Through life, it gets damaged and depleted, and then requires healing to become strong and whole again.

Dark Energy

The famous physicist Albert Einstein developed his theory of general relativity to solve limitations in our understanding of gravity—this is the force that holds us to the Earth and stops us from floating into space; it's why everything falls to the ground and is what keeps the planets orbiting the Sun.

There's just one problem, which is that there simply isn't enough mass (weight) in the Universe for this to work. Einstein realized that there must be more mass creating a greater force that as yet we cannot see or measure. This led to the concept of "dark matter" and "dark energy." (They are referred to as being "dark" only because we cannot see them—there's no inference of evil to the darkness.) Later, physicists calculated how much dark matter and dark energy there is in the Universe.

Only about 5 percent of the Universe is visible matter, which we can see and record. The other 95 percent of the cosmos is composed of dark matter (27 percent) and dark energy (68 percent). Maybe this invisible energy makes up the piece of us that we call the human soul or spirit. Maybe it doesn't die along with our physical body which we can see. Maybe it's that fleeting glimpse of something you notice out of the corner of your eye when you feel a presence, but when you turn, there's no one there. Maybe it connects us through time and space to our past lives (see pages 76–85), and maybe our future…

The Body's Energy

As we have discussed, your body has its own energy system. This is made up of meridians, which are channels for *chi* (see page 113) to flow through your body; chakras, which are your body's fundamental energy hot spots; and the aura, which is an energy field that surrounds the body.

Aura

The aura is made up of several layers, and everyone's aura is unique to them. Your aura protects you energetically and allows you to exchange energy and communicate with the world around you. Everything that ever goes wrong in the body occurs in the aura first. Whether that is tiny stresses building up over time, which affect you physically, emotionally, and mentally, or a bus hitting you suddenly, it's happened in your aura first.

You can sense another person's (or animal's) aura; you might feel a presence when they come into a room before you see them. And when you watch a genuine star performing live on stage, you can sense their aura reaching out to fill the theater, auditorium, or arena.

The aura is a protective energy field surrounding the body.

PRACTICAL EXERCISE:
SENSE THE AURA

It is possible to sense the aura with your hands, but it's much easier to do this with a crystal pendulum. Here are exercises for both options. You will need a willing friend who should stand still, away from any walls.

WITH A PENDULUM

1 Assuming you know your pendulum's "yes" and "no" responses (if not, see page 99), hold your pendulum in one hand about 2–3 in (5–8 cm) in front of your friend's heart.
2 Ask your pendulum, "Is this the *edge* of their aura?" Your pendulum will answer "no." If the pendulum doesn't move, then ground yourself and start again. You could hold hematite in your other hand to help keep you grounded (see page 100).
3 Once you have your "no" response, keep the question in your mind, then slowly move away from your friend until your pendulum changes its response to show you a "yes." This has identified the *edge* of their aura.

The aura's size is naturally continuously changing, so don't expect it to show exactly the same position if you try this again.

Lapis lazuli pendulum

WITH YOUR HANDS

1 First, shake your hands vigorously.

2 Stand in front of your friend, about 1–2 yards (90–180 cm) beyond the edge of the aura you have just found with the pendulum. (If you haven't tried the pendulum method, just stand 1–2 yards (90–180 cm) away from your friend.)

3 Hold out your hands, with palms facing your friend at about heart level, and very slowly move toward them until you feel a difference. Some people feel this as a temperature change (getting warmer or cooler), tingles in their palms, or pressure as they slowly advance.

When you have sensed your friend's aura, swap over and let your friend have a go at sensing yours—first with the pendulum, then with their hands.

Chakras

The chakras are the body's energy "hot spots." They don't exist as solid, physical entities, but you can feel them and sense when they are out of kilter. Chakras are the main places in which you exchange energy with the outside world; they are the link between your physical body and your aura.

There are many different, mainly yogic, systems of chakras, with the major chakras ranging in number from 3 to 24. There are hundreds of minor chakras, too. Different traditions have varying views on the importance of some of the chakras and denoting them as major or minor. For simplicity, we will focus on the seven major chakra system, which is most followed in the West.

When your chakras are functioning well, there is a continuous healthy flow of *chi* between you and your surroundings. When a chakra isn't working as well as it should, we might say that it's blocked. It isn't totally blocked; it's more that the energy isn't flowing as well as it could. If this persists, it will lead to disease, which may manifest on any or several levels—physically, emotionally, mentally, or spiritually. By following a simple exercise to keep your chakras balanced (see box opposite), you are more likely to remain healthy and heal quicker from any injury on any level.

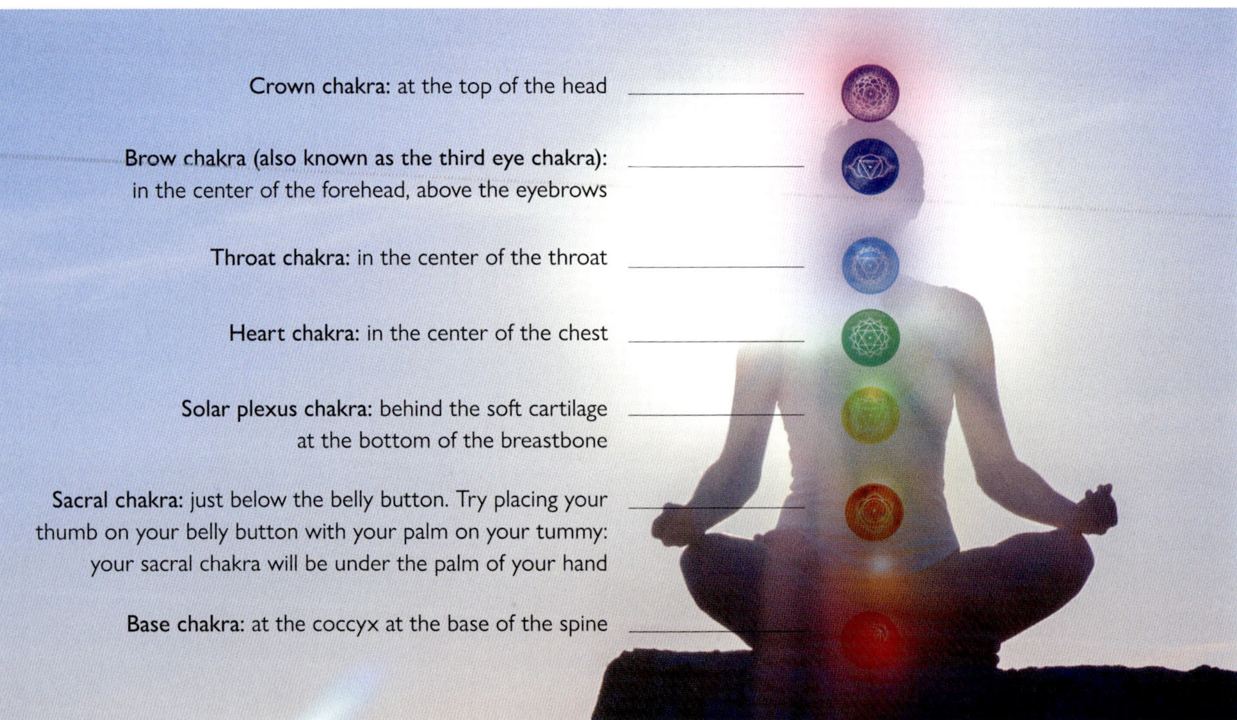

PRACTICAL EXERCISE:
BALANCE YOUR CHAKRAS

You will need seven crystals to help you balance your seven chakras. You may choose to work with a "standard" crystal chakra set (see page 120) or select the crystals yourself—they don't have to match the chakra colors. (I put "standard" in quotation marks because the standard varies from one person or school to another, but all will work.) It's best to choose a time of the day when you can do this self-healing crystal treatment regularly, such as in the early morning or late evening, so it can become part of your routine. This exercise has two parts.

For the first part of the exercise, place the seven crystals directly on or around the chakra points to facilitate healing.

1 Prepare a comfortable space. You might like some meditative music, dimmed lighting or candles, a cozy blanket, and some incense or fragranced oil. All of this is lovely but not essential to the process.

2 Lie down on your back and place the seven crystals on the corresponding chakras of your body. It is easier to start from the base chakra and work your way up.

3 Be still and relax. You can lie like this for 10–20 minutes, or much longer if you prefer. (You could even place the crystals on your body just before you go to sleep.) Don't worry if any crystals fall off—leave them there and relax.

The second part of this exercise is to keep your chakra crystals with you all day long. You can place them in your pocket or bra, or wear them in a neck pouch or as jewelry. This will help to keep your energy in balance during the ups and downs of everyday life.

Remember to cleanse your crystals after you have worked with them (see pages 128–132).

Standard Chakra Crystal Set

Chakra	Associated Concepts	Associated Crystal
Crown	Spirituality, connection to Universe, imagination, awareness, optimism	Amethyst
Brow	Mind, ideas, thoughts, dreams, psychic abilities	Lapis lazuli
Throat	Communication, expression, responsibility, freedom, leadership	Blue lace agate
Heart	Love, safety, trust, adventure, relationships	Malachite
Solar plexus	Physical center, personal power, emotions	Citrine
Sacral	Connection to other people, creativity, energy, confidence	Carnelian
Base	Survival, health, abundance, connection to Earth, moving forward in life	Red jasper

Beings of Light

Spiritual scripture from religions and oral traditions around the world use descriptions such as "beings of light," "we come from the light," "we are the light of the world," "we return to the light" when we die, "God's light shines through us," "lead us to the light," "divine light" that is within everyone, "enlightenment," "to find the light," "let there be light," "festival of light," "Buddhas of light," "inner light," "light of divine consciousness," "illumination on the path," "cross of pure light," "light of the human soul," and many other examples.

Traditional healing methods often work by supporting the innate human ability for our bodies to heal themselves and by empowering the "light" within us. Up until relatively recently, science considered this a simple story with no factual foundation. However, quantum physics confirms that our ancestors were correct! We are indeed beings of light. We are physically constructed from particles of light, which make up all the atoms and molecules in our bodies. Our DNA, our cells, and our organs, including our brains, are all made of these particles of light.

Quartz crystals can focus light. Try the practical exercise on the following page to see for yourself.

PRACTICAL EXERCISE:
QUARTZ FOCUSING LIGHT

In a brightly lit room, hold a natural quartz crystal in one hand, about 1–2 in (2–5 cm) above the open palm of your other hand, with the crystal's termination pointing toward your palm.

Move the crystal slowly in a clockwise circle above your hand. Look at your palm and you will see a point (or line or area) of light moving on your palm as the crystal circles your hand. The light may be directly under the crystal or offset to one side. Sometimes the light is clear to see; sometimes you need to look more closely. This changes with different crystals depending on the angle of the crystal lattice and the crystal's termination. The brightness of the light will also differ from one crystal to another. The crystal is picking up the light in the room and focusing it on your palm. Don't be surprised if you start to notice a feeling in your hand, such as a tingling, warmth, or coolness, as the light moves around your palm.

Remember to cleanse your quartz crystal after you have worked with it (see pages 128–132).

Crystal Healing in Our World Today

Crystals can be such powerful tools for healing your body, emotions, mind, and soul. They work holistically, so can aid all of these areas (which are often considered as separate by conventional medicine) as one. Crystals not only heal but also affect how we feel and our responses to the world around us. They can support us when we feel down and need a helping hand, and help to boost our natural abilities when we're doing well. If simply by adding beauty, crystals improve the quality of our lives.

Physical Healing

Crystals can help your body to repair itself physically because they are able to channel energy, and balancing the energy in a damaged area allows the body's natural healing processes to work as well as possible. Crystals will not do something that the body cannot do. If someone has unfortunately lost an arm, then just like the body, crystals will not be able to grow the arm back. But what crystals *can* do is help to speed up the body's natural processes. For example, if someone has a bruise on their arm, their body will naturally heal the bruise

NOTE

Practical crystal healing is too big a subject to cover in detail in this book, so I offer a brief, but comprehensive, introduction to some of the ideas of modern crystal healing. I have written several other books covering the subject in detail (see the Resources section on page 138).

by itself. However, by working with the right crystals—in this case, clear quartz, citrine, aventurine, and fluorite—the body will heal the bruise quicker. With just a little bit of crystalline help, the body can self-heal remarkably well.

Quartz Crystal Points

As discussed on page 122, quartz crystals can focus and direct light, and we as human beings are made of light (see page 121). So, naturally, if you can work with quartz to focus more light on an area of the body that is damaged or painful, it should help to speed up the body's natural healing process and relieve pain. The technique is exactly the same as that described on page 122 where you employed quartz to focus light onto the palm of your hand. When you do it this time, hold the quartz so it is pointing toward the affected area and focus your mind on repairing the damage or reducing the pain.

Citrine

Citrine is another crystal that can speed up the body's repair from any physical injury. Citrine works by helping you absorb nutrients from food. Nutrients are the building blocks of your body, so, put simply, if you are absorbing more nutrients, you have more material to repair the damage, and it is easier for your body's organic healing process to take effect.

Hold a citrine crystal on or near the affected area for 20 minutes or so daily until it is completely repaired. If you like, you could tape the crystal on or near to the area for a longer period of time. I usually suggest that the crystal is in place for 12 hours, then removed for 12 hours. You can have the citrine taped to you during the daytime or nighttime—whichever suits your lifestyle better.

Citrine

Emotional Healing

Our emotions play a big role in linking the physical and mental aspects of healing. When someone feels positive, they physically heal quicker. By ignoring the mental state of patients, medical practitioners may fail to get the best results they could from their practice.

Emotions can be triggered by physical events, such as trauma or hormones; mental events, such as happiness or fear; and external factors, such as bereavement and travel. All these factors can have positive or negative effects on the individual and will vary from one person to another. For example, one person may thrive on stress, while another may suffer anything from mild to extremely negative symptoms. However, the person who thrives may well be building up harmful energy in tiny doses with long-term detrimental effects.

Crystals can impact our emotions. If you are already feeling well, crystals could help you to feel even better!

Stress

As a crystal healer (and I'm sure any therapist, doctor, or health professional would agree), I can guarantee that every client I see will be stressed in some way, and that their stress will be the root cause of their symptoms, be they physical, emotional, mental, or spiritual. Crystals can be worked with to help treat stress. It's best to select crystals simply by trusting your intuition or by asking your pendulum (see pages 99–100), but sometimes it can be helpful to have a guide, so I offer some suggestions on the next page.

Green calcite

Green Calcite

Wonderfully calming and relaxing, green calcite relieves anxiety and panic attacks almost instantly. You can also try apatite, aventurine, azurite/malachite, black tourmaline, blue quartz, other varieties of calcite, chrysoprase, citrine, green moss agate, and labradorite. Each works subtly differently to relieve anxiety.

Imperial topaz (top), rhodonite (left), and rhodochrosite (right)

Imperial Topaz, Rhodonite, and Rhodochrosite

The combination of these three crystals can help you to cope with twenty-first-century stress—the type that is caused by running around, trying to do too much, and be everywhere for everyone all the time.

Aquamarine (top), emerald (left), and beryl (right)

The Beryl Family

Aquamarine, beryl, emerald, and morganite are all calming.

Morganite

Silver Topaz

This crystal can help you to see and understand the real source of your troubles.

Silver topaz

Tourmaline

Giving you a feeling of protection and inner strength, tourmaline is my go-to crystal to alleviate worry about other people's opinions of you. Tourmaline, blue jade, celestite, lepidolite in quartz, muscovite, Picasso stone, and tiger's eye can also all help you to worry less—the single most useless human occupation!

Tourmaline

All these crystals will help to bring quick stress relief. Hold any or all of them whenever your stresses challenge you. Alternatively, carry one or more of them with you in a bag or pocket, or wear it as jewelry. For this to work most effectively, it is essential to carry, wear, or be near to the crystal all the time, day and night. The crystal will work subtly, yet continuously, on the underlying cause(s) of your stress.

PRACTICAL EXERCISE:

ACTIVATE AND ENHANCE YOUR CRYSTALS WITH A QUARTZ CRYSTAL

You can enhance the power of your crystals by activating them with a quartz crystal. To do this, simply place the crystal(s) you want to work with on a flat surface or hold it in your nondominant hand. Hold a quartz crystal in your dominant hand, about 2 in (5 cm) above the other crystal(s). With the quartz's termination pointing down, move it slowly in a clockwise direction for a minute or two. If this is difficult to do yourself (if the crystals are already placed on your body, for example), ask your partner or a friend to help. When you have finished working with your crystals, remember to cleanse them (see pages 128–132).

Crystal healers use many more techniques—some ancient, some modern—to harness and help to direct a crystal's innate healing energy to areas where it is needed within the body and to the aura surrounding the physical body.

How to Cleanse Crystals

It is important to cleanse crystals after you have worked with them. With every type of healing, there is always an exchange of energy. With crystals, a simplified way of looking at this is that the crystal gives you healthy energy and takes away unhealthy energy. If you then work with this crystal, either on yourself or someone else, the first thing it does is give out the unhelpful energy it's picked up, then replace it with good energy from you or the other person! There are many ways to cleanse crystals. Here are some different methods, although this is not an exhaustive list.

Sound

Tingsha are also known as Tibetan bells.

In most situations, this is my preferred cleansing method. I use *tingsha*, sometimes called Tibetan bells, which are two cymbals traditionally tied together with a strip of leather, although you sometimes see them tied with cotton or silk cord. They are made of several different metals—usually five or seven—and when struck together, the sound waves vibrate through the metal lattice, reverberating for a significant time, the best-quality ones for several minutes. The sound literally "shakes" the energy free and it is released from the crystal. This method is simple, clean, easily portable, and you can use it to cleanse many crystals at the same time—and I have a lot of crystals! In a crystal healing session with a client, I will usually work with upward of 50–100 crystals.

Running Water

One of the most traditional methods of cleansing a crystal is to hold it under running water. The idea is to wash away all the gunky, sticky, dull energy, leaving your crystal revitalized and sparkly again. I use this technique to cleanse myself after a working day—perhaps after seeing clients with deep-rooted issues or just lots of customers in the crystal showroom with disparate energy. When I get home, I shower and let the water wash away all the unwanted energy that's stuck to my aura during the day. The same principle applies to cleansing crystals with water.

Ideally, you would use fresh, flowing water from the top of a mountain or underneath a waterfall. If this is available to you locally then that's the best choice. But do be practical because you need to cleanse your crystals regularly; tap water works perfectly well. Some crystals, such as water-soluble varieties, are not suitable for this method, so make sure to check first.

Moonlight

The Moon has a powerful influence on everything; it moves oceans and affects your hormones and your brain. Putting crystals out in the moonlight to be cleansed is a lovely practice, which you could make a regular monthly ritual. To do this, take the crystals outside into your garden or backyard at nighttime and sit with them for a few minutes. Think about adding your intent to the energy of the Moon—this will enhance the power of the cleansing process amazingly, and also helps you to let go of any stress you might be holding on to. If the weather is bad, or you don't have a backyard, use a windowsill or a table by a window instead.

Crystals can be cleansed by moonlight.

Smudging

The burning of incense or herbs to spiritually cleanse objects and spaces runs through religious beliefs and traditions around the world. Examples include the use of sage in some Native American ceremonies, frankincense in Christian, Islamic, and Jewish traditions, and sandalwood in Buddhist and Hindu practices. As a generalization, the metaphysical community has adopted the use of North American sage smudge sticks (see practical exercise box opposite) and South American *palo santo* wood (Spanish for "holy wood"), which is sourced mainly from Ecuador and Peru, as their favorite cleansing incenses.

You can cleanse crystals with the smoke that is produced by burning smudge sticks.

TIP

There's a difference between cleansing and cleaning. Cleaning is a physical process, which should be practiced in addition to cleansing. In particular, make sure your crystals aren't dusty. Dust is held to a crystal by an electrostatic charge, and one of the ways in which crystals work is by balancing electrical charges in your cells. So, any dust on a crystal will affect its efficacy. To remove dust, lightly brush your crystals with a soft brush—a makeup brush or small paintbrush is ideal. Do this regularly to avoid a buildup of dust.

PRACTICAL EXERCISE:
SMUDGING CEREMONY

A smudging ceremony inspired by Native American traditions is a beautiful way to cleanse crystals. You will need a sage smudge stick (a bundle of sage), an abalone (or similarly large) seashell, a feather, and matches or a lighter. The sage represents Earth, the abalone shell signifies Water, the smoke embodies Fire, and the feather symbolizes Air.

You will also need a flat, fireproof surface and some water or other extinguisher nearby for safety. Always make sure you are in a well-ventilated space.

1 Hold the smudge stick in one hand over the abalone shell and light the sage. The shell stops any embers dropping to the ground and damaging floor coverings or setting fires.

2 Holding the feather in your other hand, use it to waft the smoke from the smudge stick over your crystals. It is the smoke that is cleansing, and the feather traditionally guides your prayers to spirit.

3 When you have finished, it is best to extinguish the smudge stick in sand or earth. Putting it out in water is effective but makes it difficult to relight and reuse.

You can also use this method to cleanse your home, office, chairs—in fact, anything at all.

Abalone shell

Other Crystals

Selenite

Certain crystals, such as selenite and amethyst, can cleanse other crystals. Simply place your crystals on a flat plate of selenite overnight to cleanse them. Since selenite is a cleansing crystal, many crystal healers work with it at the end of a treatment to clear their client's aura of any remaining unwanted energies and/or themselves to shed any that they may have picked up from their client.

Alternatively, place your crystals on an amethyst bed. This is a bit like sending a tired friend on vacation, so they can come back refreshed. I'm often asked how long you should leave crystals on an amethyst bed and I always say the same thing—it's just like a vacation; sometimes you only need a day in the country or a weekend city break, but other times a week in Florida, a couple of weeks in the South of France, or a month in the Caribbean is what's needed! Keep an eye on your crystals and you will notice when they have recharged.

Amethyst

Remember that you will need to cleanse your selenite or amethyst occasionally, too, because they will be exchanging their lovely, cleansed energy with the energy that your other crystals need to let go of!

Rebirth

This practice involves burying crystals in the ground and leaving them for a period of time, then digging them up later when they will be reborn, free of the energies that were clouding their own. A great time to bury crystals is on a full moon (a period of completion). Dig them up on the following new moon, which is the time of new beginnings. It's a good idea to mark the spot where you have buried your crystals, so that you can find them later—and if you have a dog, don't let it see you bury the crystals as it might dig them up and rebury them somewhere else!

Conclusion: Our Crystal Future

To bring the book to a close, I'd like to give you a glimpse into what humanity's crystal future may look like. Developments in technology and medicine move quickly. Imagine how crystal energy will play a part in this in the future…

Waking Up

It is morning. You wake up, thanks to the slightly warm feeling in the back of your hand as one of the microscopic memory dots in your quartz crystal implant switches itself on at the perfect time, as it does every day. Reaching to your nightstand, you feel for your crystals. Your garnet crystal gives a subtle boost to your physical energy.

Crystal bracelets

Jo comes in with breakfast. Jo always knows what you want to eat before you know you need it, because it reads information from the quartz crystal chip in your hand. The chip monitors every aspect of your health, so your food is prepared to suit your exact dietary needs. Jo's crystalline brain has calculated and placed the precise dietary requirements (PDR) into the polytetrafluoroethylene and quartz crystal cooking units to cook your food perfectly to your taste. This cookware is easy to clean and hard-wearing, and has eliminated all illness caused by ineffective food hygiene.

After having breakfast, you realize you'll need to be very aware of people's energies at your meeting in Paris later, so you apply your lapis lazuli blue eye shadow to give your psychic powers an edge. You then put several crystal bracelets on your wrists. Everyone has at least a hundred different crystal bracelets and wears a selection of these each day, ever since the top universities and institutions finished a combined research program into the efficacy of crystal healing. This has proved so effective that it has vastly reduced visits to health professionals and working days lost to mental health issues.

Just as you're leaving your house, you notice the bowl of crystals by your front door and for no particular reason pick up an amethyst crystal and pop it in your pocket.

Travel and Work

In your driveway is your new crystal solar-powered car, which also makes use of rubies in its laser-tracking system, quartz lenses in the high-quality cameras, and, of course, crystals and minerals in the computer system that drives the car itself. With AI-driven cars, there are far fewer driver fatalities.

At your meditation class, you sit, breathe, and start to relax. Your teacher has chosen a celestite crystal for you. He explains how it links to intuition, awareness, and dreams and goals, which is all ideal for your upcoming Paris meeting. The teacher always seems to select the right crystal for each person in the group.

After your class, you arrive at your office for that Paris appointment. Of course, you could have taken the 30-minute space flight from New York to Paris, but no one really has in-person business meetings anymore. As you sit at your desk, the AI system instantly recognizes you through its liquid crystal technology. You used to need the fingerprint sensor, but now the high-security systems have retina readers, using phosphorescent crystals, to identify the unique pattern of blood vessels in the back of your eye. In a fraction of a second your computer comes to life. As you put on your virtual reality headset, you are effectively transported to Paris as your meeting begins.

Blue celestite

Your meeting goes fabulously well, so you gather your nearby Paris team together to head to your favorite restaurant. As you enter, you scan the quartz crystal chip in the back of your hand, which confirms your identity and that you have enough money in your account to pay for the meal, as well as checking your body chemistry, so the restaurant can prepare the perfect meal to match your tastes and PDR.

Socializing

After dinner, you all want the party to continue. You book four limousine taxis to take the group to the hottest nightclub in the city! Driverless cars had not been popular, but with smiling robot drivers there's a feeling of normality. Of course, the robots don't actually drive the taxis—the cars drive themselves, obviously—but it's nice for people to see a face behind the wheel.

When you arrive at the nightclub, once again you scan the back of your hand to confirm your identity, and the scanner also evaluates your body chemistry. This is the real crystal magic! The scanner uses germanium photodiodes to detect the codes in your chip, and then, for your personal safety, a quartz crystal records your every movement. Your code is passed through an X-ray crystallography machine, revealing the three-dimensional structure of the proteins in your blood. A balanced drink is then created for you that matches your PDR and which will also lighten your mood, reduce your blood pressure, relieve stress, bring mental balance, and taste absolutely amazing.

At some stage, one of your team complains of a headache. You remember the amethyst crystal you picked up from the bowl by your front door on the way out this morning. You give it to her, remembering how, when a crystal calls to you, there is always a reason; even when you do not personally need the crystal, it will help someone you know or meet during the day. A while later, you hit the dance floor where you can dance the night away with some amazing androids! You see your team member dancing with one of the androids, and realize how well that amethyst helped clear her headache. The revelry continues well into the early hours.

It is morning. You wake up, thanks to the slightly warm feeling in the back of your hand as one of the microscopic memory dots in your quartz crystal implant switches itself on at the perfect time, as it does every day.

Amethyst

PRACTICAL EXERCISE:
CREATE YOUR OWN CRYSTAL FUTURE

What would you like to see in your future? Some people want to physically change things by inventing new ideas and technologies. Others might manifest their dreams by focusing on their desires. For this exercise, you will need one hand-sized or larger quartz crystal, preferably bought especially for this purpose or that you haven't worked with before, and six smaller ones.

1 Look at all the crystals you have around your home. How could they help you in your everyday life? Then look around again and notice all the technology in your home, from refrigerators and freezers to computers and entertainment systems. Think for a moment about what each of these could do if they all spoke to one other. Then imagine your world 5, 10, 20, or 50 years from now.

2 Hold the larger quartz crystal and take a few slow, deep breaths. Each time you breathe in, feel your chest rise as your energy gets lighter. As you exhale, imagine you are blowing out any thoughts that make you feel heavy. Keep breathing like this until you feel an inner smile rising within you.

3 Picture your future world. Whatever you want is important here—don't concern yourself with what you think others might want. Hold the image in your mind for as long as you can.

4 At night, just before you go to sleep, hold your larger quartz crystal and recall your experience. Then make a quartz crystal grid by placing the six smaller quartz crystals so they are all pointing toward the center in a circle around the larger crystal. Ask the crystal grid to manifest your future.

5 Repeat this each day for as long as you wish: hold the larger crystal, visualize your desired future, and place it back in the crystal grid.

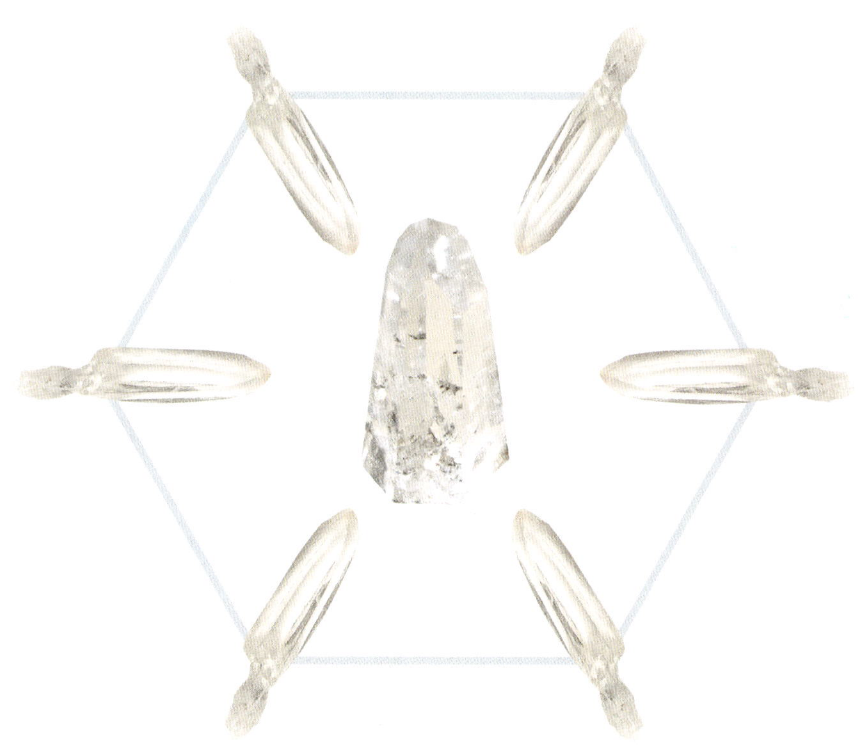

Resources and Further Reading

Philip Permutt has written many other books about crystals, published by CICO Books. Here is a selection:

- *The Crystal Healer: Crystal prescriptions that will change your life forever* (2007)
- *The Book of Crystal Grids: A practical guide to achieving your dreams* (2017)
- *The Crystal Healer: Volume 2: Harness the power of crystal energy* (2018)
- *The Modern Guide to Crystal Chakra Healing: Energy medicine for mind, body, and spirit* (2022)
- *Crystal Connections: Understand the messages of 101 essential crystals and how to connect with their wisdom* (2023)
- *Crystals For Everyday Living: Bring happiness to your home, achieve your goals, and enhance every element of your well-being* (2024)

An ephemeris (see page 46) can be accessed at: https://horoscopes.astro-seek.com/astrology-ephemeris-planetary-online-ephemerides

Philip's website, with an online crystal store and details of his workshops, classes, and courses, can be found at www.thecrystalhealer.co.uk. You can also follow him on Facebook (facebook.com/TheCrystalHealer), X (@CrystalHealer), and Instagram (@thecrystalhealer).

All of Philip's music (including that mentioned on page 84) is available to download or stream from all streaming services, including Amazon Music, Apple Music, YouTube, Pandora, and Spotify. It can also be downloaded from his website (link above).

Glossary

Akashic Records A library of spiritual information that exists on another plane.

Aura The subtle energy field around the body.

Chakra The Sanskrit word for "wheel." Chakras are the energy centers of the body, appearing as wheels to people who can see energy.

Chi In Chinese medicine and philosophy, *chi* is the energy or life force of the Universe, believed to flow round the body and to be present in all living things. Other cultures call *chi* by different names. For example, *ki* (Japan) and *prana* (India).

Clairvoyance The ability to see psychic information.

Crust The top or outer layer. Crystals occurring as crusts are growing on the surface of a rock or mineral.

Distant healing The process of sending healing energy, good thoughts, or prayers to a person who is not physically present. Also known as absent healing or remote healing.

Druse A surface crust of small crystals on a rock of the same or a different mineral. A crystal that exhibits druse can be described as "drusy."

Elixir A crystal elixir is water in which a crystal has been immersed.

Energy A supply or source of power: electrical, nuclear, mechanical, or subtle, such as *chi*.

Feldspar A group of silicate minerals.

Fire A play of color caused by dispersion of light within a crystal, such as that shown by diamonds. Fire opal does not necessarily exhibit fire, but occurs in colors of fire: reds, oranges, yellows. Opal does not display true fire but a play of light caused by the scattering of light by microscopic silica spheres in the opal structure.

Hominins: Collective term for modern humans (*Homo sapiens*) and our extinct human ancestors and relatives.

Hypnosis A state of consciousness where a person is highly responsive to suggestion or direction.

Inclusion A mineral found within the structure of a different mineral.

Iridescence The colors that appear inside a crystal due to either the diffraction or refraction of light within the crystalline structure.

Karma/karmic process/karmic healing Karma equals action or deed. Also refers to cause and effect and specifically to how the actions of an individual can/will affect their future. Karmic healing is about healing karma from past lives or this life, so you do not take it with you into the next life, meaning it cannot influence the next life.

Manifestation The bringing of your dreams, desires, or goals into physical reality.

Mass Matter that has no definable crystalline structure. When the term massive is used, it refers to this rather than to the size of the crystal.

Meridian An energy pathway through the body. Meridians carry *chi* in the same way that veins and arteries carry blood.

Past-life recall/regression Recollection of a previous existence before your current life. Regression is the shamanic or therapeutic process of facilitating past-life recall.

Prismatic Describes a crystal with faces that are similar in size and shape and run parallel to an axis; the ends are rectilinear and similar in size and shape. For example, a triangular prismatic crystal has two triangular ends joined by three rectangular faces, while a hexagonal prismatic crystal has two hexagonal ends connected by six rectangular faces.

Psychic abilities These include intuition or gut feelings, clairaudience (the ability to hear psychic information), clairsentience (the ability to sense psychic energies), clairvoyance (see page 139), sensing energies and auras, seeing and interpreting auras, telepathy, extrasensory perception, and increased insight through divination and tarot card readings.

Rebirth A fresh start after the death of a dream, goal, idea, project, or era of your life, leading to a new beginning.

Record keeper Describes a crystal with raised triangles on the face of the termination.

Refraction/double refraction Refraction is the bending of light as it moves from one medium to another, such as from air into a crystal. Double refraction (also known as birefringence) occurs when a single ray of light splits into two when it moves from one medium to another. This happens when light enters an optical calcite crystal, for example.

Shamanic healing An umbrella term covering a multitude of ancient forms of healing, all of which are linked to nature. One of the oldest forms of traditional healing.

Soul pools The belief that our soul is part of a pool of conscious energy and individual souls are connected. When we die, our soul returns to the pool of energy, sharing its experience and lessons from this life.

Spirit guides The beings or energies of departed souls who impart information, knowledge, and wisdom to help you on your path.

Striations Parallel grooves or markings along the length of a crystals.

Subtle energy Energy that is outside the known electromagnetic spectrum and therefore not easily detected.

Tabular Describes crystals that are broad and flat; sometimes shortened to "tabby."

Termination The end of a crystal formed by the facets or faces making up the point. Note that a few varieties of crystal have flat terminations, such as some tourmaline and spodumene crystals.

Totem animals Animal spirits or characteristics that help to guide you on your path in life.

Translucent Describes a material that light can pass through but any objects on the other side are not clear.

Transparent Describes a material you can see through, which could be described as "crystal clear."

Index

Page references in *italics* refer to glossary entries.

Picture Credits

Key: t = top; c = center; b = bottom; l = left; r = right

Photography by Roy Palmer, Geoff Dann, James Gardiner, Tino Tedaldi (p. 128) and David Mereweather (p. 129) and illustration by Clare Nicholas, Trina Dalziel (pp. 98–9), and Nina Hunter (p. 47), all © CICO Books, except as stated below.

Practical Exercise borders (pp. 27, 42–3, 62–3, 65, 69, 70–1, 73 , 84–5, 90–1, 94–5, 99, 102–3, 116–17, 119, 122, 127, 131, 136–7): Adobe Stock/releon8211

Full-page backgrounds (pp. 1–3, 8–9, 28–9, 50–1, 74–5, 104–5): Adobe Stock/Наталья Босяк

Box frames (pp. 31, 66–7, 83, 88, 101): Adobe Stock/andras_csontos

p. 1 Adobe Stock/Sam/indysystem/sakkmesterke; p. 3 Adobe Stock/HISTOCK/Hakim; p. 6 Adobe Stock/Microgen; p. 11l Adobe Stock/spiritofamerica; p. 11r Adobe Stock/viktoriya89; p. 12t Adobe Stock/Montree; p. 12b Adobe Stock/bidaya; p. 13 Adobe Stock/benevolente; p. 14 Adobe Stock/Kim; p. 15t Adobe Stock/dimamoroz; p. 15br Adobe Stock/rana/Hakim; p. 16l Alamy Stock Photo/Len Collection; p. 17r Adobe Stock/W.Scott McGill; p. 18 Adobe Stock/Valerie2000; p. 19 Adobe Stock/tilialucida; p. 20t Adobe Stock/WavebreakMediaMicro; p. 20b Adobe Stock/Adrio; p. 21 Adobe Stock/razihusin/Hakim; p. 22 Adobe Stock/Gorodenkoff; p. 23tl Adobe Stock/Siwakorn1933; p. 23tr Adobe Stock/NNL_STUDIO; p. 24l Adobe Stock/Panitan; p. 25 Adobe Stock/dimazel; p. 26 Adobe Stock/Michael Flippo; p. 31 Adobe Stock/ImageKing/Hakim; p. 33 Adobe Stock/DolonChapa/Hakim; p. 35 Adobe Stock/ZethX/Hakim; p. 36b Adobe Stock/warren_price; p. 37b Adobe Stock/migfoto; p. 39 Adobe Stock/Felix Pergande; p. 40b Adobe Stock/tashka2000; p. 41 Adobe Stock/mahir; p. 43 Adobe Stock/Microgen/Hakim; p. 44 (pearl) Adobe Stock/shlyapanama; p. 45 Adobe Stock/Aquir; p. 46 Adobe Stock/Viktoria; pp. 48–9t Adobe Stock/urvana; p. 49 (planetary symbols) Adobe Stock/Зоя Лунёва; p. 52 Adobe Stock/Indri; p. 54 Adobe Stock/MheeP/Hakim; p. 55 Adobe Stock/Archivist; p. 59 Adobe Stock/RaNy; p. 60t Adobe Stock/reichdernatur; p. 60b Adobe Stock/pisan Thailand; p. 63 Adobe Stock/NpicArt; p. 64t Adobe Stock/reichdernatur; p. 64b Adobe Stock/Thiago/Sunny/Hakim; p. 65t Adobe Stock/Thiago; p. 65b Philip Permutt; p. 67 Adobe Stock/Jag_cz; p. 68t Adobe Stock/reichdernatur; p. 69t Adobe Stock/reichdernatur; p. 70t Philip Permutt; p. 70b Adobe Stock/reichdernatur; p. 71t Adobe Stock/HISTOCK/Hakim; p. 71b Adobe Stock/Firman Dasmir/Hakim; p. 72b Adobe Stock/Kanthowork; p. 76 Adobe Stock/sajar; p. 77 Adobe Stock/Kim; p. 78 Adobe Stock/rolffimages; p. 80b Adobe Stock/alphaspirit/Felix Pergande/trihubova; p. 85 Adobe Stock/AI Photo Stock/Hakim; p. 87 Adobe Stock/ipopba; p. 89 Adobe Stock/SeanPavonePhoto; p. 91 Adobe Stock/Thiago; p. 92 Adobe Stock/Mnt; p. 94 Adobe Stock/zah108; p. 96 Adobe Stock/Alev; p. 97 Adobe Stock/elen31; p. 100b Adobe Stock/Preeya; p. 102 Adobe Stock/vannet/YiuCheung; p. 103t Adobe Stock/vannet/YiuCheung; p. 103b Adobe Stock/reichdernatur; p. 106 Adobe Stock/Lyubov; p. 107 Adobe Stock/BOOCYS; p. 108 Adobe Stock/solidmaks; p. 109 Adobe Stock/vencav/Hakim; p. 111 Adobe Stock/peopleimages.com; p. 112 Adobe Stock/nimon_t; p. 113 Adobe Stock/furyon; p. 114 Adobe Stock/sakkmesterke; p. 115 Adobe Stock/Oleg Zaharov; p. 117 Adobe Stock/Iryna/Hakim; p. 118 Adobe Stock/Dmytro Flisak/reichdernatur; p. 120 (chakra symbols) Adobe Stock/reichdernatur; p. 121 Adobe Stock/OS; p. 122 Adobe Stock/Sam/indysystem/sakkmesterke; p. 125 Adobe Stock/Ruben/Hakim; p. 127 Adobe Stock/Nikki Zalewski; p. 130 Adobe Stock/Premium_art/Hakim; p. 131t Adobe Stock/Farid; p. 133 Adobe Stock/Oporty786; p. 136 Adobe Stock/BrilliantPixels/Hakim

Acknowledgments

Having recovered from lung cancer at the beginning of this year (2025), my thank-yous include some new people. Firstly, every one of the hundreds of people who sent me distant healing from around the world, as well as the surgeons, nurses, and all the other specialists and ancillary staff at Harefield Hospital.

Thanks to my fabulous friend Nicci Roscoe for all your help and support and for keeping everything going during my convalescence, and for being an inspiration as well as in-house editor.

For each book I write, I find myself thanking my staff at The Crystal Healer Crystal Showroom, affectionately known as the Crystal Healer Helpers. But it really is true that without Claire and Becky, and Rachel who handles the social media, finding the time to write this book would have been impossible. I am always grateful to all my clients, customers, students, and friends who inspire me to take the next steps on this glittering crystal path and discover more about the wondrous world of the Stone People every day and help to create the wealth of experience I share with you.

Thanks to the people at CICO Books who turn my words into magical books, particularly Carmel Edmonds who helped get this book off the ground and Imogen Valler-Miles for managing some of my verbosity. Thank you, Cindy Richards, for having faith in the beginning, all those years ago.

Finally, the people who inspired me to write: my father Cyril, American crystal healer Melody, and Ian, who knows why.